Impact of Family Planning Programs on Fertility

Phillips Cutright
Frederick S. Jaffe

The Praeger Special Studies program—
utilizing the most modern and efficient book
production techniques and a selective
worldwide distribution network—makes
available to the academic, government, and
business communities significant, timely
research in U.S. and international economic, social, and political development.

Impact of Family Planning
Programs on Fertility
The U.S. Experience

PRAEGER SPECIAL STUDIES IN U.S. ECONOMIC, SOCIAL, AND POLITICAL ISSUES

Praeger Publishers   New York   Washington   London

Library of Congress Cataloging in Publication Data

Cutright, Phillips, 1930-
  Impact of family planning programs on fertility.

  (Praeger special studies on U.S. economic, social,
and political issues)
  Includes bibliographical references.
  1. Birth control—United States. 2. Fertility,
Human. 3. Birth control—Research—United States.
I. Jaffe, Frederick S., joint author. II. Title.
HQ766.5.U5C87   301.32'1   76-12847
ISBN 0-275-23350-2

PRAEGER PUBLISHERS
111 Fourth Avenue, New York, N.Y. 10003, U.S.A.

Published in the United States of America in 1977
by Praeger Publishers, Inc.

Printed in the United States of America

Planning for this research was partially supported by the General Service Foundation. The study itself was supported by the Center for Population Research, National Institute of Child Health and Human Development, under Contract NO1-HD-3-2722, with additional support from Indiana University and the Alan Guttmacher Institute. The Alan Guttmacher Institute provided much of the base data used for this research. Tapes of the 1969 and 1971 studies of family planning needs and services by county were made available by J. G. Dryfoos, who also prepared 1970–75 service data and estimates of need and population for use in chapter 7. The 1969 files were constructed for use in the publication of *Need for Subsidized Family Planning Services: United States, Each State and County, 1969* under contract B89-4588 with the Office of Economic Opportunity, Washington, D.C. The 1971 files were constructed for use in the publication of *Need for Subsidized Family Planning Services: United States, Each State and County, 1971* under contract HSM 110-71-280 with the National Center for Family Planning Services, DHEW. Additional 1970 census data were produced by the Alan Guttmacher Institute staff.

M. Hout, a graduate student in the department of sociology, Indiana University, Bloomington, was largely responsible for the analysis of the determinants of program enrollment (chapter 3). This work is a valuable addition to our knowledge about family planning program development. We deeply appreciate Hout's contribution, which required a large input of both talent and time. An unpublished analysis of the determinants of program enrollment ("Components of successful county family planning programs: a suggested model for program development") by D. R. Weintraub and B. L. Nelson of the Alan Guttmacher Institute was incorporated in the theoretical framework of Hout's study.

Merging information from three separate data sources to the county level, checking the accuracy of the data, and preparing tapes compatible with the computer facilities of Indiana University was undertaken by G. Eubanks, Applied Personnel Inc., Bloomington, Indiana.

Professor E. Jackson, department of sociology, Indiana University, was our statistical consultant. Direct processing of data (aside from chapter 3, which was done by Hout) was performed by W. R. Kelly, a graduate student in the department of sociology, Indiana University. Kelly's contribution was performed largely on his own time.

The 1970 National Fertility Study data used to assess the plausibility of our estimates of potential program impact, were all women in need served (chapter 5), were supplied by Charles F. Westoff and Lois Paul, Office of Population Research, Princeton University.

An earlier version of this study was read by Professor Westoff; John Ross of the International Institute for the Study of Human Reproduction, Columbia University; and Ilene Bernstein of Indiana University. We are indebted to them for their critical comments and suggestions. The final responsibility for the findings and conclusions, of course, remains with the authors.

We also acknowledge helpful work in editorial matters, as well as expert typing, by A. W. Hite, assistant to Professor Cutright, and H. Bemporad, senior administrative assistant to Mr. Jaffe.

CONTENTS

LIST OF TABLES

LIST OF FIGURES

LIST OF ABBREVIATIONS

AFDC	Aid to Families with Dependent Children
CEB	children ever born
CPI	Consumer Price Index
DHEW	Department of Health, Education and Welfare
IUD	intrauterine device
MCA	multiple-classification analysis
NCHS	National Center for Health Statistics
NFS	National Fertility Study
NRSFPS	National Reporting System for Family Planning Services
SAU	statistical analysis unit
SES	socioeconomic status
SMSA	Standard Metropolitan Statistical Area

Do family planning programs reduce fertility, independent of other social, economic, and cultural factors that affect childbearing? Have the social programs initiated in the United States during the 1960s "failed" to achieve their objectives?

The first question lies at the heart of the international debate over population policy and was a dominant theme in the United Nations World Population Conference held at Bucharest, Romania, in 1974.[1] The second is a major issue in current disputes over social policy in the United States.

Answers to these questions require rigorous evaluation of the effects of program interventions. Since family planning programs are designed to assist individuals to prevent unwanted pregnancy, program effects should be measurable in fertility change. Numerous studies have sought to evaluate the demographic impact of family planning programs in less developed countries, but the results are sometimes ambiguous because of inadequate data as well as the inherent difficulties in isolating the effects of a single program from other, simultaneous social changes.[2] In the United States, where the available data generally are more adequate, few attempts have thus far been made to assess the impact of the national program.[3]

The availability of 1969 county-level statistics from family planning clinics and 1970 county-level census data on women of reproductive age and their children provided a unique opportunity to attempt a systematic national evaluation. Accordingly, this study, the Family Planning Program (FPP) Impact Study, was undertaken to determine whether family planning clinic programs have had a demonstrable impact, net of other factors, on the fertility of U.S. women.

NOTES

1. Challenges to the effectiveness of family planning programs can be found in K. Davis, "Population policy: will current programs succeed?" *Science,* 158:730, 1967; J. Blake, "Population policy for Americans: is the government being misled?" *Science,* 164:522, 1969; and P. Hauser, "Population: more than family planning," *Journal of Medical Education,* 44:20, November 1969. Contrary views are in B. Berelson, "Beyond family planning," *Science,* 163:533, 1969, in regard to less developed countries; and, in regard to the United States, O. Harkavy, F. S. Jaffe, and S. M. Wishik, "Family planning and public policy: who is misleading whom?" *Science,* 165:367, 1969; L. Bumpass and C. F. Westoff, "The 'perfect contraceptive' population," *Science,* 169:117, 1970; and F. S. Jaffe, "Towards the reduction of unwanted pregnancy," *Science,* 174:119, 1971. For a summary of the international debate, see B. Berelson, *The Great Debate Over Population Policy* (New York: Population Council, 1975).

2. For a useful summary of the extensive evaluation literature, see R. Freedman and B. Berelson, "The record of family planning programs," *Studies in Family Planning,* 7:1, January 1976. Studies employing approaches somewhat comparable with this book—multiple-regression analysis of small areas—include A. I. Hermalin, "Taiwan: an area analysis of the effect of acceptances on fertility," *Studies in Family Planning,* 1(33):7, August 1968; and "Taiwan: appraising the effect of a family planning program through areal analysis," Taiwan Population Studies Working Paper no. 14 (Ann Arbor: University of Michigan Population Studies Center, 1971); T. P. Schultz, *Effectiveness of Family Planning in Taiwan: A Methodology for Program Evaluation* (Santa Monica, Calif.: RAND Corporation, 1969); R. Repetto, "A case study of the Madras vasectomy program," *Studies in Family Planning,* 1(31):8, May 1968; G. B. Simmons, *The Indian Investment in Family Planning* (New York: Population Council, 1971); and J. Riew, "Some factors associated with the cost of the family planning program in Korea" (University Park: Pennsylvania State University, 1971). (Mimeographed.)

3. Most U.S. studies have been local in focus, but two that employ areal analyses are R. W. Rochat, C. W. Tyler, and A. K. Schoenbucher, "The effect of family planning in Georgia on fertility in selected rural counties," *Advances in Planning Parenthood* 6 (New York: Excerpta Medical Foundation, 1971); and N. H. Wright, "Vital statistics and census tract data used to evaluate family planning," *Public Health Report,* 85(5):383, 1970.

Impact of Family Planning Programs on Fertility

1

THE DEVELOPMENT OF
U.S. FAMILY PLANNING
PROGRAMS AND THE GOALS
OF THIS RESEARCH

Organized family planning clinic programs in the United States have grown substantially since federal funds to support these services became available in the mid-1960s. In 1965 clinic programs are estimated to have provided services to about 450,000 individuals. By 1975 the number had increased to more than 3.8 million, based on data reported primarily by the National Reporting System for Family Planning Services (NRSFPS) and similar state and local computerized systems (see Table 1.1). From 1969 through 1972, organized programs sustained a 32 percent average annual rate of growth in patients served, and the rate increased to 38 percent during 1972. These years coincided with congressional and executive actions to assign priority to the program and substantially to increase federal appropriations for family planning projects. In 1973, 1974, and 1975 the annual rate of growth declined to 18, 6, and 16 percent, respectively, following the leveling off of federal appropriations.

This study was undertaken to determine whether these programs have had a demonstrable impact, independent of other factors, on the fertility of those who participated in the program. Inherent difficulties arise in isolating program effects from the variety of nonprogram variables that can influence fertility, and these difficulties have precluded efforts to evaluate systematically the demographic impact of U.S. programs. The coincidence of a decennial census in 1970 and the availability of national county-by-county studies of organized family planning clinic programs in 1969 provided a unique opportunity to attempt such a systematic national evaluation. The results of the study are presented in this book.

At the outset we will present selected information on the scope and characteristics of organized family planning programs, utilizing data for various recent years to characterize the programs, and on fertility trends in the period under study.

TABLE 1.1

Estimated Number of Patients in Organized Family Planning Programs: Fiscal 1965-Fiscal 1975

Fiscal Year	Patients (1,000)	Annual Rate of Growth (Percent)
1965	450	—
1966	540	20
1967	690	28
1968	863	25
1969	1,070	24
1970	1,410	32
1971	1,889	34
1972	2,612	38
1973	3,089	18
1974	3,282	6
1975	3,813	16

Note: Fiscal years run July 1-June 30.

Sources: Fiscal 1965-67, unpublished estimates by the Planned Parenthood Federation of America; fiscal 1968-73, Department of Health, Education and Welfare, Office of Population Affairs, *A Five Year Plan for Family Planning Services and Population Research–Fourth Progress Report* (Washington, D.C.: U.S. Government Printing Office, 1975), p. 39a; fiscal 1974-75, Alan Guttmacher Institute, *Data and Analyses for 1976 Revision of DHEW Five Year Plan for Family Planning Services* (New York: Alan Guttmacher Institute, 1976).

THE SCOPE OF ORGANIZED FAMILY PLANNING PROGRAMS

In the United States the norm for delivery of most health services, including family planning, is the physician in private practice. Organized clinic programs for the provision of family planning services serve persons who are unable to secure them from private physicians for economic and other reasons. These programs are set up under a variety of administrative auspices that include local health departments, governmental and private hospitals, and voluntary organizations such as Planned Parenthood, community groups, and neighborhood health centers. Regardless of auspices, a program typically serves patients through scheduled clinic sessions at which physicians or physician equivalents are present; physicians usually work part-time in family planning programs, staffing clinic sessions only, while other personnel may or may not be employed full-time. Some of these programs provide only family planning services, but most offer other health services as well (particularly maternal health services). A family planning service generally consists of medical services (medical examination, instruction, and prescription), educational services (such as patient recruitment and discussion of the relative merits of different methods), and social services. Some programs include medical services for infertility, but the overwhelming majority of patients are concerned with contraception.

The programs are financed with varying mixes of government funds, private contributions, and fees from patients. Since the mid-1960s governmental funds have increased most rapidly of these sources; the bulk of these funds are federal, authorized first under the 1967 Social Security amendments and the Economic Opportunity Act, and later by the Family Planning Services and Population Research Act of 1970 (P.L. 91-572). Some programs offer services free of charge, while others charge fees that represent all or part of the cost. Some utilize defined levels to establish eligibility, with the fee for service related to family income, while others serve anyone who comes, regardless of income.

Comparatively little is known about the delivery of medical services by physicians in private practice, and family planning conforms to this general pattern. Much more is known about the delivery of health services through institutional providers, and that is also true of family planning. Therefore, evaluation of the U.S. domestic program, must, of necessity, be limited to evaluation of organized clinic programs with diverse administrative controls, sponsorships, and institutional interests, and with little or no firm knowledge of the activities of private physicians.

Organized programs can be described in substantial detail. Their primary objective is "to enable Americans freely to determine the number and spacing of their children,"[1] with priority for serving low-income persons. As of June 30, 1974, organized family planning programs of some kind were identified in almost two-thirds of U.S. counties and were operated by nearly 3,400 different agencies—755 hospitals, 1,767 health departments, 222 Planned Parenthood affiliates, and 639 other voluntary organizations.[2]

In 1974 the median age of program patients was 23, with 85 percent below age 30. The median educational attainment was 11.2 years. Forty-five percent of patients had never had a live birth, and the mean number of children reported for all patients was 1.2; only 18 percent had three or more children. Sixty-three percent of patients were white, 33 percent black, 4 percent other. Virtually all patients had low or marginal incomes: 54 percent had incomes below the federal poverty index (an income in 1974 of $5,038 for a nonfarm family of four), 73 percent had incomes below one and one-half times the poverty index, and 86 percent had incomes below twice the poverty index.[3]

This overall picture includes considerable variation. The lion's share of patients are served by a small number of agencies in relatively few large metropolitan counties; most counties reported very small programs. Three national county studies of organized programs have assessed reported program levels against a standardized estimate of need for family planning among low-income persons.[4] The proportion of the estimated need group served, which provides a comparative measure of program enrollment, varied directly and consistently with the size of the reported caseload and of the county's population. In 1971 the variation ranged from zero percent of estimated need met in 1,344 counties with no programs to more than 50 percent of estimated need met in 169 counties.* While local variations may occur in fertility attitudes and in the sources of health care available to low-income persons that would explain part of these observed differences in utilization of family planning programs, they probably would not explain a variation this great. The more obvious explanation is that variation is primarily a function of program effort, a hypothesis that is tested in chapter 3. This factor, in turn, plays an important role in our analysis, which essentially seeks to determine whether areal differences in program enrollment are systematically related to areal differences in fertility, when sociodemographic factors are controlled.

One other dimension of the program has an important bearing on the questions we are examining. In addition to providing various health examinations and diagnostic tests, the programs serve as a channel for the distribution of the most effective means of contraception currently available. In fiscal 1974 about 34 percent of new patients used no contraceptive method at all prior to clinic enrollment and 17 percent used less effective, nonmedical methods. After enrolling in organized clinic programs, 82 percent of new patients chose oral contraceptives, intrauterine devices (IUDs) and sterilization—the three most effective current methods. (The proportion of all patients—new and continuing—using these most effective methods in fiscal 1974 was 90 percent.)[5] Since these three methods have failure rates that are only one-fourth to one-seventh those of other methods,[6] the programs clearly have been associated with a major improvement of contraceptive efficacy among large numbers of low-income and young persons.

THE PERIOD UNDER STUDY

Family planning programs can only prevent births that are unwanted (number failures) or mistimed (timing failures). A number failure is a birth not

---

*The estimate of need employed in the published report for 1971 was computed for women in families with incomes below 150 percent of poverty. In the analyses presented below, the need estimate has been computed at the 200-percent-of-poverty cutoff. As a result the ratios of patients to need presented in this study differ from those in the 1971 report.

wanted at any time; a timing failure is one that would have been preferred at a later time. If the family planning program has had an impact on fertility levels net of other factors, we would expect it to have occurred among those subgroups of the population served by the program. As we have seen, almost all patients of organized programs have low or marginal incomes below 200 percent of the federal poverty index. Women in this subgroup account for about one-third of all U.S. women of childbearing age. Given the relatively small number of patients in 1969, any program effect on fertility in this subgroup of the childbearing population is not likely to be visible in community-wide rates reflecting the total population.*

This basic consideration determined the period of our study and the research design. The 1970 census provided information, as of April 1970, that could be used to construct measures of fertility for subgroups of the childbearing population classified by socioeconomic status (SES), and these measures in turn could be related directly to the subgroups served by the program in the period immediately preceding the census enumeration. The census provided information on other factors believed to affect fertility that also could be computed for socioeconomic subgroups and used to control for nonprogram factors affecting fertility.

The best indicator of current fertility available from the census was the enumeration in April 1970 of children under one year. Such children were born between April 1969 and April 1970; and if the family planning program had an impact on this fertility measure, that impact was the program as it operated in the year prior to April 1969. Program statistics, however, were available either for calendar year 1969 or fiscal 1968 (ending June 30, 1968). After consideration the calendar year 1969 data were selected because they were more reliable at the county level and provided greater detail on some aspects of the program. (An adjustment for bias resulting from using calendar year 1969 rather than the appropriate point-in-time measure of patients is reported in Chapter 2, section "Adjustment of Unstandardized Regression Coefficients Measuring Program Effects.")

We are thus examining the effects of areal differences in family planning program enrollment in 1969 on areal differences in fertility in 1969–70. Notice that our program enrollment measure reflects an early period in the growth

---

*To overcome this problem in studies of the impact of local programs, some investigators have attempted to use median income or rentals of census tracts, while others have used color-ethnic fertility measures. See, for example, P. Darney, "Fertility decline and participation in Georgia's Family Planning Program: temporal and areal associations," *Studies in Family Planning,* 6:156, June 1975. Neither procedure is entirely satisfactory—the first because of the geographic dispersion of low-income persons and the second because color is an inexact and often misleading surrogate for poverty.

of organized family planning programs in the United States. In calendar year 1969, 1.2 million were served in organized programs—about 14 percent of the estimated population of women below 200 percent of poverty in need of services. The caseload has more than tripled in subsequent years, bringing about a more even geographical distribution of the services than in 1969 (although, as noted above, they remain concentrated).

These factors have several implications for our analysis. First, we expect that because of the relatively small national caseload in 1969, if the program had an effect on fertility, it could not have been large. Second, we will be measuring the impact of the program as it existed in 1969, and not necessarily the impact of the program as it exists today. In addition to the obvious change in size of caseload and in the proportion of all low-income women of childbearing age now receiving services, other characteristics of the program in 1969 were different from those in 1974. Both the low-income composition of patients and the upgrading of contraceptive practice have been fairly constant over the years, but the proportion of patients below age 30 and those with no live births has changed significantly. The 1969 program served a caseload that was somewhat older and had more children, while in recent years the program has increasingly reached women before they have had their children. These changes, we believe, should lead to an even stronger impact on current fertility levels than are discernible in the 1969–70 data.

In one respect the timing of our study is fortuitous, because 1969 preceded the major changes in abortion laws in New York and other states that began in 1970. As a result our findings will not be distorted by the differential availability of legal abortion services in various parts of the country that was evident even after the Supreme Court's abortion decision in 1973.[7]

TRENDS IN FERTILITY

The growth of organized family planning programs occurred in a period when overall U.S. fertility was declining. Studies utilizing varying data bases have shown several important patterns within this overall decline, most of which is attributable to a reduction in unwanted and unplanned births resulting from more consistent use of contraception, greater use of the more effective contraceptive methods, and improved efficiency in their use.[8] The decline in unwanted births has been greatest among the subgroups (such as blacks and women with little education) that had previously experienced the highest unwanted rates.[9] The decline in fertility generally has been most pronounced among disadvantaged minorities and low-income groups, and among women in the lowest intervals classified by the federal poverty index.[10]

These changes have occurred during a decade marked by numerous alterations in social and economic conditions and at least two in the variables immediately related to fertility. The period is roughly coterminous with the decade in which the oral contraceptive and the IUD modernized U.S. contraceptive practice[11] and there was an increasing acceptance of the concept of governmental responsibility for the provision of family planning services, at least to low-income persons. In essence, this study was undertaken to assess the effectiveness of the latter development.

PURPOSES AND DESIGN OF THE STUDY

The major goal of the study is to evaluate the impact of differential enrollment in organized family planning programs on 1969–70 fertility rates of women with low or marginal incomes. A secondary purpose is to test the usefulness of different methodologies in assessing the demographic impact of U.S. programs.[12]

As noted above, the study is based on areal analyses. To determine program impact, the analysis would best be done with data for individuals, tracing the before-program and after-program fertility experience of patients against the fertility experience over the same time periods of women with comparable characteristics who were not participants in organized family planning programs. Such a national study could not be done because the necessary data for individuals are not available. The areal analyses employed here, while not ideal, may provide a satisfactory method of evaluating program effects.

Numerous other changes were occurring at the same time as the initiation of the program; and the purpose of the study is to measure program impact, net of other factors that might have influenced fertility in the study year. Accordingly, for each areal unit measures are computed of demographic characteristics (such as age, marital status, and population density) and socioeconomic conditions (such as labor force participation, income, and educational attainment) that affect fertility levels. Most of these variables are computed for specific subsets of the population of women of childbearing age in each areal unit, while others are computed for the area as a whole. These control variables include the level of fertility for specific subgroups of women in years prior to the time tested for program effects. Together with our areal measures of program enrollment, they form the set of independent variables that are employed in multivariate analysis to determine the effect of the program, net of other factors, on variations in areal fertility rates among low-income and marginal-income women.

The detailed methodology of the study, and the specific measures employed as independent and dependent variables and their sources, are detailed in chapter 2.

NOTES

1. Senate Committee on Labor and Public Welfare, *Report of the Secretary of Health, Education and Welfare Submitting Five-Year Plan for Family Planning Services and Population Research Programs* (Washington, D.C.: U.S. Government Printing Office, 1971), p. 77.

2. Department of Health, Education and Welfare (DHEW), Office of Population Affairs, *A Five-Year Plan for Family Planning Services and Population Research—Fourth Progress Report* (Washington, D.C.: U.S. Government Printing Office, 1975), p. 51.

3. Fiscal 1974 program data from ibid., pp. 44, 46, 47.

4. Office of Economic Opportunity, *Need for Subsidized Family Planning Services: United States, Each State and County, 1968* (Washington, D.C.: U.S. Government Printing Office, 1969); *Need for Subsidized Family Planning Services: United States, Each State and County, 1969* (Washington, D.C.: U.S. Government Printing Office, 1972); and Center for Family Planning Program Development, *Need for Subsidized Family Planning Services: United States, Each State and County, 1971* (New York: Center for Family Planning Program Development 1973).

5. DHEW, op. cit., p. 48.

6. N. B. Ryder, "Contraceptive failure in the U.S.," *Family Planning Perspectives,* 5:133, Summer 1973, Table 7.

7. C. Tietze, F. S. Jaffe, E. Weinstock, and J. Dryfoos, *Provisional Estimates of Abortion Need and Services in the Year Following the 1973 Supreme Court Decisions: United States, Each State and Metropolitan Area* (New York: Alan Guttmacher Institute, 1975).

8. C. F. Westoff, "The decline of unplanned births in the United States," *Science,* 191:38, January 9, 1976; and "The yield of the imperfect: the 1970 national fertility study," *Demography,* 12:573, November 1975; and N. B. Ryder, "Recent trends and group differences in fertility," in C. F. Westoff, ed., *Toward the End of Growth* (Englewood Cliffs, N.J.: Prentice-Hall, 1973), p. 57.

9. N. B. Ryder and C. F. Westoff, "Wanted and unwanted fertility in the United States: 1965 and 1970," in U.S. Commission on Population Growth and the American Future, *Demographic and Social Aspects of Population Growth,* Vol. I of *Commission Research Reports* (Washington, D.C.: U.S. Government Printing Office, 1972), p. 467.

10. J. Sweet, "Differentials in the rate of fertility decline: 1969–1970," *Family Planning Perspectives,* 6:103, Spring 1973; A. A. Campbell, "The role of family planning in the reduction of poverty," *Journal of Marriage and the Family,* 30:236, May 1968; and F. S. Jaffe, "Low-income families: fertility changes in the 1960s," *Family Planning Perspectives,* 4 (1):43, January 1972; "Low-income families: fertility in 1971–1972," *Family Planning Perspectives,* 6:108, Spring 1974.

11. C. F. Westoff, "The modernization of U.S. contraceptive practice," *Family Planning Perspectives,* 4 (3):9, July 1972.

12. P. Cutright, "Family planning evaluation using Census, vital and program statistics," in J. R. Udry and E. E. Huyck, eds., *The Demographic Evaluation of Domestic Family Planning Programs* (Cambridge, Mass.: Ballinger, 1975), p. 81, provides a 1973 statement of the goals, research design, and methodology of this study that may be compared with the goals, design, and methodology actually used. The 1973 procedures are little different from those followed in this report.

2

METHODOLOGY

This chapter discusses sources of data, units of analysis, the classification of women into separate groups, measurement of family planning program enrollment, and other variables used in the analysis of program effects on fertility. General methodological issues that apply to our research problems are reviewed.

UNITS OF ANALYSIS AND SOURCES OF DATA

The count of patients enrolled in organized family planning programs in the United States during the period under study was reported only by county. Accordingly, other variables had to be obtained at the county level. Data from the 1970 census measure fertility and other characteristics of subgroups of women aged 15–44 within each county, specific to age, marital status, SES, and race. Seventy-two subgroups of both white and black women were broken out (see Table 2.3 below).

Vital statistics reports of the number of 1969 births in each county, by age of mother and race, were obtained from the National Center for Health Statistics (NCHS), including both legitimate and illegitimate births in counties reporting legitimacy. Infant deaths from 1969 vital statistics by county of residence and race also were included in our files.

The third major source of county-level information was service statistics from organized family planning clinic programs and related program data, provided by the Alan Guttmacher Institute (formerly the Center for Family Planning Program Development).[1] These data included the number of patients enrolled in organized family planning programs in each county in 1969, the number and types of family planning agencies and clinic locations, and some additional information. Similar 1971 program information also was acquired from the Institute's data archives.[2]

Data from these three sources were merged for each county. Counties with fewer than 20,000 white women aged 15–44 were aggregated with contiguous counties having small populations until the total count reached 20,000. This area (whether formed from a single county or several counties) is called a statistical analysis unit (SAU). Analysis of fertility of the white population is through 778 "white" SAUs. Counties with fewer than 10,000 black women aged 15–44 were similarly aggregated with contiguous counties until (with few exceptions, see Table 2.1 below) the total count reached 10,000. Analysis of the black population is through 237 "black" SAUs. Census, vital statistics, and family planning program data were merged for each SAU. The decision to establish a different minimum number of women by race was based on rough estimates of the differential risk of poverty, by race. Because much of our analysis was to be age-specific and poverty-specific, adequate sample size within race-specific, age-specific, and poverty-specific groups was required. About 29 percent of white and 60 percent of black women 15–44 were below 200 percent of the poverty index, the cutting point employed in this analysis. The higher incidence of poverty among blacks requires a smaller total black SAU population to provide adequate numbers of women in the subgroups below the poverty cutoff. The limit of about 20,000 white and 10,000 black women aged 15–44 per SAU provides adequate sample size within most of the 72 subgroups within each SAU. Any SAU with fewer than 300 women in a subgroup is automatically eliminated from a given subgroup analysis.

TREATMENT OF STATISTICAL ANALYSIS UNITS

The mean SAU values of some characteristics will not always be similar to a national average based on counts of individuals, although the SAU is used in all analyses. To illustrate this, Table 2.1 shows the total number of women of all races aged 15–44 living in SAUs grouped by the number of counties required to provide an SAU population of adequate size. The 388 SAUs that contained only one county had a total of 29.3 million women aged 15–44, nearly 5.1 million of whom were below 200 percent of poverty and in need.*

---

*See section "Program Enrollment" for definition of "need." Estimates of need for age-race-marital status subgroups below 200 percent of poverty were weighted to produce the number of women aged 15–44 below 200 percent of the federal poverty cutoff in need of family planning services. The age, race, and marital status of patients were not available by county. For detailed need statistics see J. G. Dryfoos, "A formula for the 1970s: estimating need for subsidized Family Planning service in the United States," *Family Planning Perspectives,* 5:145–74, Summer 1973.

In single-county SAUs the ratio of patients per 1,000 women to need is 194 (column 6) when the total number of 1969 calendar-year patients in these SAUs (986,000, column 5) is compared with the total number of individuals estimated to be in need (5,081,000, column 4). However, when the ratios of patients to need in each of the 388 SAUs are averaged, the resulting mean SAU value is just 113 (column 7), well below the actual weighted ratio of 194. The difference between the weighted and mean SAU patients/need ratio persists in all classifications by number of counties; as a result the national weighted average of 144 differs sharply from the mean patients/need ratio per SAU of 82.*

Table 2.2 shows selected characteristics of the white and black SAUs grouped by the number of counties required to construct the SAU. In the upper panel, for example, the average white single-county SAU had 65,000 white women aged 15–44. Three hundred eighty-eight such SAUs existed; they have the same SAU mean patients/need ratio as in Table 2.1 because they are geographically identical and the patients/need ratio is composed of patients and women in need of all races. In column 5 the mean number of women per 1,000 classified as rural is shown; for the white SAUs the average is 416. The number of white rural residents per 1,000 women 15–44 nationally, using the individual count, is 264. The difference is that in computing the SAU mean, each SAU is counted equally, while for the national average the calculation is weighted by population size. Weighting SAUs by size is not appropriate in analyses such as those pursued in this study.

The lower panel of Table 2.2 shows similar data for black SAUs. The "Total" row shows that the mean number of black women aged 15–44 per black SAU is 20,000, although some SAUs composed of two to four counties are below our lower limit of 10,000. This discrepancy results in part from the distribution of the black population and the difficulty in finding contiguous counties with black populations. Only 1,490 counties are included in the black SAUs—less than half the total for whites. The dispersion of the black population made construction of multicounty SAUs more difficult for blacks than for whites. The mean black SAU patients/need ratio of 142 is quite close to the weighted count of 144 (Table 2.1). This occurs because blacks are concentrated in metropolitan areas that have more advanced family planning programs. In contrast with the mean SAU value of 416 rural residents per 1,000 among whites, the black figure is 239.

---

*This difference results from not weighting the patients/need ratio by population size, but does not affect the validity of results in subsequent analyses. Each SAU is treated as equal to any other SAU included in each analysis, despite differences in population size.

TABLE 2.1

Numbers of Women, Counties, SAUs, Women in Need, and 1969 Patients, by Number of Counties in the SAU: All Races, Aged 15-44, 1969-70

Number of Counties	Women 15-44 (1,000) (1)	Number of Counties (2)	Number of SAUs (3)	Women in Need (1,000) (4)	1969 Patients (1,000) (5)	CY Ratio of Patients to Need (6 = 5 ÷ 4)	Mean SAU Ratio of Patients to Need (7)
1	29,345	388	388	5,081	986	194	113
2	1,307	94	47	282	33	116	67
3-4	3,037	419	121	778	43	55	40
5-7	2,778	563	96	794	49	63	50
8-14	3,150	931	94	952	67	70	55
15-24	1,166	504	27	346	18	51	48
25-35	345	170	6	111	5	54	47
Total	41,130	3,070	779	8,353	1,201	144	82

Notes: "Women in Need" figures include only those below 200 percent of the federal poverty cutoff in need. See section "Program Enrollment" of this chapter for definition of "need." Nonwhites other than blacks are included. The patient and need totals here are slightly larger than national totals in Table 2.2 because this table includes one additional SAU and nonwhites other than blacks.

Source: Family Planning Program (FPP) Impact Study.

TABLE 2.2

Characteristics of SAUs, by Racial Classification and Number of Counties in SAU: 1969 and 1970

Number of Counties per SAU	SAU Mean Number of Women 15-44 (1,000) (1)	Number of Counties (2)	Number of SAUs (3)	Mean SAU Ratio of Patients to Need × 1000 (4)	Rural per 1,000 (5)
White SAUs					
1	65	388	388	113	248
2	26	94	47	67	476
3-4	23	416	120	40	583
5-7	26	563	96	50	631
8-14	29	931	94	55	606
15-24	36	504	27	48	604
25-35	54	170	6	47	611
Total	46	3,067	778*	82	416
Black SAUs					
1	31	90	90	201	95
2	6	12	6	109	321
3-4	8	96	28	114	276
5-7	11	215	36	124	307
8-14	15	480	45	95	323
15-24	18	535	30	97	398
25-35	19	62	2	52	502
Total	20	1,490	237	142	239

*The total count of white SAUs is one less than the 779 SAUs in Table 2.1 and chapter 3, where vital statistics data are not used. Vital statistics data for one SAU were unreadable.
Source: FPP Impact Study.

CLASSIFICATION OF WOMEN

Table 2.3 shows the 72 types of women for whom various measures of fertility were computed. Some subgroups are not examined in this report. The rationale behind these divisions is related to population size within subgroups of an SAU, practical matters of how much data could be examined, and the limitations imposed on the study by its specific goals and data.

The data base began with exact 1970 census counts in each county of the more than 41 million U.S. women aged 15–44, by age, race, marital status, and poverty and income status.[3] These women of reproductive age were divided

TABLE 2.3

Subgroups of Women for Whom Separate White and Black Fertility Measures Are Available: 1969 or 1970

File	Age	Marital Status	Poverty Level	File	Age	Marital Status	Percent of Median Income
1	15-44	All*	All	37	15-44	All*	Under
2	15-19			38	15-19		50 percent
3	20-29			39	20-29		of median
4	30-44	↓		40	30-44	↓	income
5	15-44	Married,		41	15-44	Married,	
6	15-19	with		42	15-19	with	
7	20-29	spouse		43	20-29	spouse	
8	30-44	↓		44	30-44	↓	
9	15-44	Never		45	15-44	Never	
10	15-19	married		46	15-19	married	
11	20-29			47	20-29		
12	30-44	↓	↓	48	30-44	↓	↓
13	15-44	All*	Below	49	15-44	All*	50-99 percent
14	15-19		200 percent	50	15-19		of median
15	20-29		of poverty	51	20-29		income
16	30-44	↓		52	30-44	↓	
17	15-44	Married,		53	15-44	Married,	
18	15-19	with		54	15-19	with	
19	20-29	spouse		55	20-29	spouse	
20	30-44	↓		56	30-44	↓	
21	15-44	Never		57	15-44	Never	
22	15-19	married		58	15-19	married	
23	20-29			59	20-29		
24	30-44	↓	↓	60	30-44	↓	↓
25	15-44	All*	Above	61	15-44	All*	100 percent
26	15-19		200 percent	62	15-19		of or higher
27	20-29		of poverty	63	20-29		than median
28	30-44	↓		64	30-44	↓	income
29	15-44	Married,		65	15-44	Married,	
30	15-19	with		66	15-19	with	
31	20-29	spouse		67	20-29	spouse	
32	30-44	↓		68	30-44	↓	
33	15-44	Never		69	15-44	Never	
34	15-19	married		70	15-19	married	
35	20-29			71	20-29		
36	30-44	↓	↓	72	30-44	↓	↓

*"All" includes separated, widowed, and divorced women.
Note: Data from NCHS for 1969 can be applied to files 1-12 only.
Source: FPP Impact Study.

into only two poverty levels—above and below 200 percent of the federal poverty index. Family income in 1969, adjusted for family size, allowed multiple poverty classifications. The 200-percent-of-poverty cutoff was selected because virtually all patients in organized family planning programs in 1969 had incomes below this level.* The influence of family planning programs on fertility would, therefore, be reflected directly in the fertility rates of women who participate in the programs.† Because the fertility of women above 200 percent of poverty is not likely to be directly affected, development of fertility measures specific to poverty level should allow program effects to emerge, if they exist.

Because poverty indexes are a function of both family income and family size, fertility rates also were computed for women classified by family income alone, and separate analyses of program effects were run. The purpose of these analyses was to serve as a check on those utilizing the poverty index and to test the extent of bias introduced by the fact that family size is a factor in its construction. Families with less than half of 1969 U.S. median family income, those with 50–99 percent of the median, and families above the median were examined separately.

Three age groups were used: women 15–19, 20–29, and 30–44. These broad age groups were required to sustain adequate sample size within SAUs. They also roughly correspond to "natural" age groupings related to childbearing—initiation and premarital sexual experience, the prime childbearing years, and the period when many women have completed their families.

Women also were classified by marital status. Women in all marital statuses and married, spouse-present women could be classified by SES and census-reported children under one year for these groups. Fertility measures specific to SES could, therefore, be developed for these groups; and they receive the bulk of our attention. The census did not separately report children under one year whose mothers were never married, separated, widowed, or divorced.

Only white and black women were included because too few nonwhites other than blacks were available to sustain analysis at the SAU level. All analyses are specific to race because some variables have different effects on

---

*Available data on the income of patients served in organized family planning programs in 1969 indicate that 84 to 94 percent of patients had incomes below 200 percent of poverty. See Center for Family Planning Program Development, *Data and Analyses for 1973 Revision of DHEW Five-Year Plan for Family Planning Services* (New York: Center for Family Planning Program Development, 1973), Table 4, p. 11.

†The fertility of those who do not participate could be indirectly influenced and reduced by the legitimizing effect of a government-sponsored program or other factors, but these effects are difficult to measure. See F. S. Jaffe, "Issues in the demographic evaluation of domestic family planning programs," in J. R. Udry and E. E. Huyck, eds., *The Demographic Evaluation of Domestic Family Planning Programs* (Cambridge, Mass.: Ballinger, 1975), p. 19.

white and black fertility. Failure to examine the data separately by race would confuse rather than clarify the results. Separate analyses show whether the program affects only whites, only blacks, or both groups.

INDEPENDENT VARIABLES

Program Enrollment

Program enrollment is measured in each SAU by the number of patients in organized family planning clinic programs per 1,000 women below 200 percent of poverty who are estimated to be at risk of unwanted pregnancy and in need of family planning services. The count of patients used in the numerator is a summary count for each county of reported caseloads of all identified provider agencies for calendar year 1969. The estimate of need for family planning, used in the denominator, is derived from application of an estimating procedure to exact counts from the 1970 census of women aged 15–44 in each county; the procedure adjusts these counts to remove women who are sterile, sexually inactive, pregnant, or seeking to become pregnant, leaving in the estimate only those who are at risk of unwanted pregnancy.[4] Neither numerator nor denominator in 1969 is specific to age, race, or marital status. This measure is labeled "program enrollment."

Interpreting an Imperfect Measure of Program Enrollment

The number of 1969 patients in organized family planning programs per 1,000 women in need below 200 percent of poverty is specific only to women aged 15–44. Both numerator and denominator include black and white, young and old, married and unmarried. From fragmentary sources reporting characteristics of patients in 1969, we estimated the age and racial distribution of patients and compared this distribution with the age and racial distribution of women estimated to be in need of family planning to gauge whether particular subgroups were overrepresented or underrepresented among patients. If some subgroups were overrepresented or underrepresented in the caseload, biases will occur in the resulting estimates of program effects when the aggregate measure of program activity is used.

While the 1969 patient data are far from conclusive, they indicate that women aged 15–19 and 20–29 were overrepresented as patients: the proportions of patients in these age groups were greater than their proportions of women in need. In contrast, women aged 30–44 were underrepresented in the caseload. A similar comparison indicates that in 1969 whites were slightly underrepresented, and nonwhites overrepresented, as patients.

These conclusions generally agree with the impressions of family planning administrators and analysts that even in 1969 younger women were overrepresented relative to the distribution of women in need. Our analysis showed, however, that very small errors in the estimates of either the number in need or of patients in a subgroup can lead to very large differences in the comparison of the proportion in need to the proportion who were patients. Although in theory these comparisons would offer a means of correcting the deficiencies of an imperfect measure of program enrollment, we decided not to pursue them because of the uncertainty surrounding the fragmentary 1969 data on patient characteristics. To adjust for bias, the degree of measurement error for subgroups in the comparison of the proportion in need to the proportion who were patients would have to be very small, or the adjustment could introduce estimates of program effects that are less accurate than the unadjusted estimates. Because the 1969 patient data could not be properly evaluated for representativeness and measurement error for subgroups was likely to be large, we used the unadjusted coefficients of the program enrollment measure for all subgroups. This decision means that program effects may be inflated in some subgroups and underestimated in others.[5]

Although the program enrollment measure cannot be broken to fit whites and blacks separately, we provide a separate analysis of whites living in predominantly white SAUs as well as of whites living in racially mixed SAUs. In "white SAUs" nearly all patients, as well as women in need, are white. A comparable analysis of blacks is not possible.

Other Independent Variables

The remaining independent variables are taken from the 1970 census and are introduced to control for nonprogram factors affecting fertility, thus reducing the likelihood of attributing spurious effects to our measure of program activity.

Population Density

The density of total 1970 population per square mile was our initial measure of population density. Density is related to the costs of children, availability of health resources, and other factors of urban life that depress fertility. The following list of measures of density illustrates alternative measures of this concept:

- Population/square mile = density
- Log (population/square mile) = log density
- 1/(population/square mile) = reciprocal of density
- Log of reciprocal of density = space

When the traditional measure of density (population/square mile) is plotted against some measure of fertility, such as children ever born (CEB), we expect CEB to decline as density increases. But beyond a certain point fertility will not continue to decline, despite further increases in density. Couples will have fewer children under crowded conditions, but they will have some. This results in a curvilinear relationship between density and fertility, rather than a linear relationship. Since the statistical models we use assume linear relationships, the density measure can be transformed by taking its natural logarithm. The correlation of log density with fertility should be larger than the correlation with the untransformed density measure. This expectation is confirmed. For example, among whites aged 15–44 in all poverty and marital status groups, the correlation of density with children ever born is –.53; when logged, this correlation increases to –.64, a substantial gain.

A potential flaw in the density measure is that it has the same people in the numerator that other variables in our equations have in their denominators.[6] This may lead to a spurious correlation of density with fertility. The problem was corrected by using the logarithm of the reciprocal of population divided by square miles (the fourth item in the above list). Compared with a correlation of –.645 between log density and white children ever born, the correlation of the log of the reciprocal is .639. The only important difference is a change of sign. Measures of people per square miles generally are negatively related to fertility; measures of space (square miles to people) take positive signs. The second density measure we label "log density," the fourth we label "space."

Low Education

The number of women per 1,000 in a subgroup with fewer than eight completed years of school is a measure of low education. This cutting point can be applied to younger as well as older age groups. Women with few years of school tend to have higher levels of fertility than those with more years of school. This variable is labeled "low education."

Migration

The number of women per 1,000 in a subgroup who resided outside the 1970 county of residence in 1965 is our measure of migration. High rates of in-migration may be related to economic opportunities for women, but among married women it probably is related to their husbands' job opportunities. Net of other factors, high rates of in-migration may increase marital fertility because of the positive effects of husband's income on fertility. On the other hand, the childless or those with smaller families may be more likely to migrate than those with children (or many children), and high rates of in-migration might conceivably lower the number of CEB in an SAU through this effect. Introduction of the migration measure controls these effects. This variable is labeled "migration."

Never-Married Status

The number of never-married women per 1,000 women by age, race, and economic status is a proxy for age at marriage when used in analysis of marital fertility. It is a direct control for marital status in analyses of fertility among women in all marital statuses. For annual marital fertility rates we expect that high proportions of never-married women will be positively related to annual marital fertility because the never-married measure is a proxy for marital duration. Areas with a high proportion of single women are areas in which married women have been married a relatively short time and their annual fertility rate might, therefore, be expected to be higher than the rate for married women in areas with an earlier age at marriage. This variable is labeled "never married."

In-School Status

The number per 1,000 women enrolled in school in a subgroup controls differences among SAUs related to concentrations of younger women in school. Because so few women aged 30 and older are in school, the variable is omitted from analyses of older age groups. It is labeled "in school."

Labor Force

The number of women in the labor force per 1,000 in a subgroup is a proxy for female opportunity costs related to having children. Areas with labor markets employing women will tend to have more women at work and lower fertility rates. Because lower fertility can also be a cause of higher rates of female labor force participation, models of reciprocal effects between fertility and labor force participation are discussed below (see "Recursive and Non-recursive Models"). This measure is labeled "labor force."

Age Group 20–29

The number of women aged 20–29 per 1,000 women aged 15–44 by race, marital status, and SES controls age structure effects when the 15–44 age group is examined. High proportions aged 20–29 should be related to high annual fertility rates, and to lower rates of children ever born among married women. This variable is labeled "age 20–29."

Parity

To control factors that affect fertility but are not included in the above set of independent variables, measures of fertility prior to 1969 within subgroups were constructed. If programs tend to be located in areas with low or high fertility, but the lower or higher fertility of these areas is not fully captured by our set of independent variables, introducing a direct measure of prior fertility should control the risk of reporting spurious program effects.

Two measures are used. The number of children under one year per 1,000 women in a subgroup reported by the census is subtracted from the number of children ever born per 1,000 women in the same subgroup to yield the mean number of children born prior to April 1969 per 1,000 women in a given marital status, age, race, and socioeconomic group. This variable is labeled "parity 1969."

A similar variable is based on vital statistics data: the 1969 general or age-specific fertility rate from vital statistics can be subtracted from CEB for women of all marital statuses to yield the mean number of CEB prior to January 1, 1969. Since the CEB measure includes children born after January 1, 1970, the measure is basically the same as the parity estimate from the census. This measure of parity is not specific to socioeconomic subgroups and is labeled "parity 1969 N."

DEPENDENT VARIABLES

Vital Statistics Fertility Rates

Race-specific general fertility rates relate 1969 births reported by vital statistics to the population of white and black women aged 15–44 in 1970. Age-specific fertility rates for 1969 also are available by race from vital statistics.

Vital statistics counts of legitimate and illegitimate births were recorded for SAUs reporting the legitimacy of 1969 births. Marital fertility rates for these selected SAUs and methodological details concerning legitimacy are examined in Appendix A.

Census Fertility Measures

Census measures of fertility include CEB per 1,000 women by age, race, marital status, and SES. This variable is labeled "CEB." Our measures of parity prior to 1969 are, of course, dependent on the census report of children ever born.

For women in all marital statuses and for married, spouse-present women, the census reported the number of children under one year at the time of the 1970 census (April 15, 1970). Our proxy for the general fertility rate based on census data is the number of children under one year per 1,000 women aged 15–44 in all marital statuses, while the proxy for the marital fertility rate is the number of children under one year per 1,000 married, spouse-present wives aged 15–44. Both measures are available for age and race subgroups, and can be specified to the socioeconomic group from which family planning patients are recruited.(The impact of measurement error on this variable in testing program effects is examined in Appendix A). This variable is labeled "children under one year."

The final fertility measure from the census—the number of women per 1,000 in the subgroup who are childless—also can be specified to race, age, marital status, and socioeconomic group. This variable is labeled "childless."

Table 2.4 summarizes the types of measures commonly used in this study. The label used in identifying variables is followed by the operational definition of the variable. Some variables (for example, agencies, locations, visits, doctors, space, and program enrollment) are SAU characteristics that do not vary with the subgroup under analysis, while most of the others are specific to each subgroup.

ISSUES IN STATISTICAL PROCEDURE AND INTERPRETATION

Determining Which Multivariate Statistical Method Should Be Used

Ordinary linear multiple-regression analysis is the method used in this study to estimate program effects. We first examine alternative techniques of handling several variables simultaneously and then discuss whether ordinary linear multiple-regression analysis is appropriate for solving the problems at hand.

Traditional multivariate cross-tabular techniques physically divide units of analysis into two or more groups. Each of these groups is again divided into

TABLE 2.4

Summary of Variables: Labels and Definitions

Label	Construction and Definition
I. Measuring 1969 program enrollment	
1. Program enrollment	Number of patients in organized family planning programs in 1969 per 1,000 women in need in 1970
2. Need	Number of women below 200 percent of poverty who are sexually active, fecund, and not pregnant or planning pregnancy
II. Family planning program activity	
1. Agencies	Number of agencies directly or indirectly providing family planning services
2. Agentypes	Number of types of agencies providing family planning services in an area; the four types are health departments, hospitals, Planned Parenthood affiliates, and other
3. Locations	The number of clinic locations providing family planning services
III. Other health care measures	
1. Doctors	Number of primary-care physicians and osteopaths per 1,000 women aged 15-44 in 1969
2. Visits	Number of visits to outpatient clinics in hospitals providing family planning services per 1,000 visits to outpatient clinics in all hospitals; visits are not necessarily for the purpose of family planning
3. Infant Mortality Rate (IMR)	Infant deaths in 1969 per 1,000 births recorded by vital statistics in 1969
IV. Demographic and economic characteristics	
1. Age 20-29	Number of women aged 20-29 per 1,000 women aged 15-44 in 1970
2. Density	Log density: log of total 1970 population/square mile. Space: log of the reciprocal of log density
3. Low education	Number of women with fewer than eight completed years of school in 1970 per 1,000 women
4. Migration	Number of women per 1,000 1970 residents living outside their 1970 county of residence in 1965
5. White	Number of white women per 1,000 women aged 15-44
6. Rural	Number of women living in rural areas per 1,000 women aged 15-44
7. Never married	Number of never-married women in 1970 per 1,000 women—a proxy for age at first marriage
8. Low income	Number of women in families with income below 50 percent of U.S. median family income in 1969 per 1,000 women; median family income for all families in the United States in 1969 was $9,433, so the cutoff for this variable was a family income of $4,716

Label	Construction and Definition
9. Public assistance	Number of women receiving public assistance in 1970 per 1,000 women below 200 percent of poverty
10. In school	Number enrolled in school in 1970 per 1,000 women
11. Labor force	Number in the labor force in 1970 per 1,000 women
V. Fertility measures	
1. Children ever born (CEB)	Total children ever born per 1,000 women in 1970
2. Children under one year	Children under one year at time of 1970 census per 1,000 women
3. Parity 1969	The number of children ever born minus the number of children under one year per 1,000 women in April 1970
4. Childless	The number of women with zero children ever born per 1,000 women
5. General fertility rate (GFR)	The number of 1969 vital statistics births per 1,000 women aged 15-44 reported by the census in 1970
6. Age-specific fertility rate (ASFR)	Number of 1969 vital statistics births per 1,000 women of a given age in 1970 per 1,000 women of the same age
7. Marital fertility rate (MFR)	The number of 1969 legitimate births reported by vital statistics per 1,000 married, spouse-present wives reported by the census in 1970
8. Parity 1969 N	CEB minus 1969 GFR, or CEB minus an ASFR for a given age-race group.

two or more groups, and analysis of differences on a dependent variable within cells begins. This method is of little value when multiple factors are known to affect the dependent variable. After the first two or three physical controls are placed on the data, cells have too few cases for meaningful analysis unless the sample is very large. Even with a large sample the number of statistical comparisons possible in a succession of multicelled tables defies comprehensible conclusions. Further, when the effects being sought are small, there is substantial risk that they will go undiscovered. In this study, for example, if one compared SAUs having no patients with SAUs in which all wives in need were served by the family planning program, the range of plausible reductions in fertility rates in different subgroups would be 28 to 231 births per 1,000 wives, which are estimates of number and timing failures in the various subgroups derived from the 1970 National Fertility Study (see Tables 5.12 and 5.13).

We considered using multiple-classification analysis, a multiple-regression technique in which categories of independent variables are created and, within each category, an adjusted deviation from the grand mean is generated. Although this form of analysis is attractive, in our case its weakness is similar to the weakness of cross-tabular analysis: the reliability of the estimate of program effect for a given category of program enrollment is no better than the number of SAUs contained within that category.

Table 2.5 displays the distribution of SAUs by level of program enrollment in 1969. In neither the white nor the black distribution do we find sample size large enough to permit reliable multiple-classification analysis that would compare varying categories of program enrollment and produce reliable estimates of net effects of program enrollment related to such categories. If program enrollment reduces fertility, ordinary least-squares regression analysis should provide more reliable estimates of these effects than multiple-classification analysis.

TABLE 2.5

Distribution of White and Black SAUs by Program Enrollment: Calendar Year 1969

Program Enrollment	Whites in All SAUs		Blacks in All SAUs	
	Number	Cumulative Percentage	Number	Cumulative Percentage
0	189	24.3	4	1.7
1-49	243	55.4	39	18.1
50-99	121	71.0	52	40.1
100-99	128	87.5	93	79.3
200-99	35	92.0	29	91.6
300-99	50	98.5	13	97.0
400+*	12	100.0	7	100.0
Total N	778		237	

*The highest program enrollment value was 763 in one "black" SAU and 782 in one "white" SAU.
Source: FPP Impact Study.

Ordinary least-squares regression analysis is not always an appropriate multivariate method. An example is reported in chapter 3, where a more refined method was substituted. We now consider common pitfalls in ordinary least-squares regression analysis using areal data.

Ignoring Curvilinear Relationships and Heteroscedasticity

Our statistical model assumes linear relationships between independent and dependent variables. To test this assumption, scatterplots were developed of each independent variable on measures of fertility. No consistent or marked curvilinearity was observed, except for density of population (defined as population divided by square miles); when transformed to a natural logarithm, density became linear. No other variables showed marked curvilinear relationships to fertility measures.

We also developed scatterplots of the errors of prediction generated from multiple-regression equations against observed fertility values. Inspection showed no evidence indicating heteroscedasticity—the errors of prediction were scattered above and below the diagonal about equally for high, middle, and low levels of predicted fertility. This is also evidence that no marked curvilinear effects exist in the data, because the linear model predicts the high, middle, or low values of the dependent variable equally well.

Interpreting Statistics Used in Regression Analysis

For each analysis of program effects, we show the mean and standard deviation of each variable used for a given set of SAUs. Variables that are constant SAU characteristics (such as space) are omitted from later tables. Initially each subgroup in chapters 4 and 5 is analyzed in tables reporting the number of SAUs, the multiple coefficient of determination (R^2), and unstandardized partial regression coefficients for each variable. In chapter 6 the analysis omits all regression coefficients of measures other than program enrollment on fertility of women in all marital statuses.

R^2 measures the proportion of variation around the mean of the dependent variable that is related to the set of independent variables; variation ranges from 0 to 1.0. If no relationship occurred between independent and dependent variables, the value for R^2 would be O; if all the differences among SAUs on the dependent variable were related to the independent variables, R^2 would be 1.0. R^2 provides a measure of the degree to which the set of independent variables "explains" or "fits" differences among the SAUs—it does not tell us whether given independent variables have strong or weak effects on the dependent variable.

Measures of the effect of specific independent variables on fertility can be expressed in two different kinds of multiple partial-regression coefficients. Standardized partial-regression coefficients (beta weights) compare the relative importance of independent variables within a given group if all independent variables are exogenous. The independent variable with the largest beta weight (either positive or negative) is generally the most powerful, and the variable with the smallest beta weight is the least important. In substantive terms a beta coefficient of .250 means that a change of one standard deviation in the independent variable, net of the remaining variables, will be related to a change equal to 25 percent of the standard deviation in the dependent variable. If the purpose of this study were to explain fertility variation by determining the relative importance of different variables as causes of the variation, we would have to use the standardized coefficients. Our purpose, however, is not to determine whether the program had a larger or smaller effect on fertility than some other variable did, but to determine whether it had any effect at all. For this purpose the unstandardized partial-regression coefficients, which are easier to interpret, are adequate as measures of net program effects and are used in most tables.

The partial unstandardized coefficients show the net effect on the dependent variable of a one-unit change in an independent variable. For example, if the unstandardized coefficient for the program enrollment variable on a general fertility rate is −.060, this means that, net of other factors in the same equation, an increase of one patient per 1,000 women in need is related to a decline of .060 births per 1,000 women in the subgroup. Interpreting the unstandardized coefficient is made easier by converting it to larger units of change. In the above example an increase of 10 patients per 1,000 women in need would then be related to a decline of .6 births per 1,000 in the subgroup and an increase of 100 patients to 6 fewer births per 1,000, while if all women in need were patients, the net effect would be to reduce the subgroup's general fertility rate by 60. The unstandardized coefficient can be compared across age, race, or poverty groups in which the set of independent and the dependent variables are the same and are measured in the same units. Comparison of these coefficients among groups tells us whether the effect of a variable is the same or different among whites and blacks, younger versus older women, the poor and the nonpoor.

In all tables the significance level of regression coefficients is reported. Any coefficient designated as significant beyond p <.05 is at least twice its standard error. If the unstandardized coefficient is significant, the standardized coefficient also is significant.

Extrapolating Beyond Observed Data

The sign (positive or negative), size, and significance of unstandardized regression coefficients for the program enrollment variable gauge program effects on fertility. A potential weakness of our study of program effects, and one for which no solution was found, is caused by the lack of sufficient numbers of SAUs with high levels of 1969 program enrollment. The unstandardized regression coefficients measure the slope of the regression line established by existing data. They can be extrapolated to a hypothetical situation in which

500 or 1,000 women per 1,000 in need are enrolled in a program. The decimal point is merely moved, as in the example above. Indeed, we use the regression estimates to gauge hypothetical effects of a total enrollment program in 1969 in chapters 5 and 6 and extrapolate them forward in time in chapter 7 to estimate births averted by the program between 1970 and 1975. But the resulting expected effects on fertility of a program serving, for example, 800 women per 1,000 in need, are actually based on data (see Table 2.5) that estimate net effects of the 1969 program on fertility between areas with no patients and areas with relatively small patient caseloads.

In principle this difficulty could be overcome by replicating the study with program data for 1975, when the number of patients served was more than three times the number in 1969; however, data on fertility and other measures specific to socioeconomic subgroups are not available for 1975, so the study cannot be replicated. Although the magnitude of the effects of the post-1969 program on fertility cannot be derived with any precision, the program's impact in later years probably was even greater than in 1969 as a result of the increasingly younger age composition of the caseload. These factors imply only that the estimates of program effects that result from extrapolations of the observed 1969 effects are to be regarded as approximations that are, however, based on demonstrated effects, the validity of which is established basically by the weight of the evidence. We know roughly what these effects should have been in 1969 and we know which groups should have had them and which should not. We have many groups against which expected and observed estimates of program enrollment can be compared. If the weight of evidence indicates that program effects exist, they probably exist. If not, then we have no program effects. The issue of extrapolation is tested in Tables 5.12 and 5.13.

Recursive and Nonrecursive Models

Our main objective is to estimate program effects, rather than to test models of explaining causes of variation in fertility. The two problems may require different statistical models. In analysis of program effects, the principal concern is that the coefficient measuring the program's impact on fertility is neither inflated nor deflated and the remaining coefficients are of less interest. In contrast, in analysis of causes of variation in fertility, the variable measuring program effects is likely to be small and the primary interest is in the relative effect of each independent variable on fertility.

The two differing objectives determine which statistical model is appropriate for each type of study, and particularly under which conditions reciprocal relationships between independent and dependent variables can be ignored. In recursive models all independent variables are treated as exogenous causes of the dependent variable; the dependent variable is not a cause of any independent variable. In nonrecursive models one or more independent variables may be endogenous and have reciprocal effects with the dependent variable. For example, high female labor force participation rates may depress fertility, but low fertility rates may be a cause of high female labor force participation. If these two variables have reciprocal effects, the regression coefficient estimating the impact of labor force participation on fertility will be depressed in the recursive model. However, the substantive concern of this study is not whether labor force or any other variable has reciprocal effects with fertility, but whether the use of recursive models to estimate program effects on fertility is valid.

To test this, both recursive and nonrecursive models are used in Table 2.6 on data for white and black wives aged 20–29 below 200 percent of poverty. The dependent variable is the number of children under one year per 1,000 wives. Several differences occur in the independent variables between the models. First, "in school" is deleted from the nonrecursive equation to reduce its high correlation with the predicted labor force variable. This omission stablized partial-regression coefficients in the nonrecursive model. Second, "labor force" in the recursive model is the observed participation rate for each group of wives, in the nonrecursive model it is the predicted labor force participation rate for women aged 20–29 below poverty in each SAU. The predicted labor force variable is obtained from an equation in which the predicted value is a function of a constant term—the labor force participation rate of all women in the SAU—and the values for the SAU on the following exogenous variables: program enrollment, space, low education, migration, never married, in school, and a dummy variable for South versus non-South region. This is normal procedure to estimate reciprocal effects in two-stage least-squares analysis. The equations shown in the nonrecursive model are the second-stage equations. R^2 does not have the same meaning in two-stage least-squares analysis as in recursive models and is omitted.

In the upper panel of Table 2.6 all variables are significant in both the recursive and the nonrecursive models. All variables also retain the same sign in both models. The major change between the two is the size of the regression coefficients attached to the endogenous variable "labor force." In the recursive model the standardized coefficient for "labor force" is weaker than that of five of the remaining variables, and only slightly stronger than the two weakest variables. In contrast, in the nonrecursive model the standardized coefficient for "labor force" is the strongest in the model.

The second striking difference between recursive and nonrecursive models for whites is the reduction in the effect of "parity 1969" on marital fertility. The standardized coefficient for parity is the most important variable in the recursive model, but drops to third rank in the nonrecursive model. Thus, the recursive model apparently not only suppressed effects of labor force on 1969 marital fertility but also its effects on fertility before 1969. Despite the change in its relative importance, however, parity is still powerful in the nonrecursive

TABLE 2.6

Estimating Program Effects on Fertility: Recursive and Nonrecursive Models

Independent Variable	Recursive		Nonrecursive	
	Unstandard- ized Coefficient	Standard- ized Coefficient	Unstandard- ized Coefficient	Standard- ized Coefficient
White				
Program enrollment	−.054*	−.133*	−.040*	−.099*
Space	−4.910*	−.205*	−2.961*	−.123*
Low education	−.089*	−.124*	−.078*	−.109*
Migration	.065*	.217*	.063*	.209*
Never married	.162*	.370*	.158*	.358*
In school[†]	−.207*	−.217*	n.i.	n.i.
Labor force[†]	−.084*	−.146*	−.410*	−.450*
Parity 1969	.057*	.395*	.041*	.285*
Black				
Program enrollment	−.097*	−.207*	−.104*	−.210*
Space	−4.883*	−.171*	−.789	−.027
Low education	−.009	−.012	−.066	−.086
Migration	.060	.163	.010	.029
Never married	.179*	.205*	.177*	.211*
In school[†]	.090	.037	n.i.	n.i.
Labor force[†]	−.017	−.037	−.247*	−.279*
Parity 1969	.027*	.156*	.025*	.146*

$*p < .05$

[†] See text for discussion of these variables. Number of SAUs was 778 in white, and 223 in black, analyses.

Note: Regression on children under one year per 1,000 wives aged 20-29 below 200 percent of poverty, 1970.

n.i. = not included in equation.

Source: FPP Impact Study.

model. When one compares the two models, the coefficients for "low education," "migration," and "never married" show little change. The regression coefficients for "space" and "program enrollment" decline, but both variables continue to have significant negative effects on white fertility in the nonrecursive model.

Among blacks three of the four variables significant in the recursive model remain significant in the nonrecursive one, "space" becoming insignificant. "Labor force" achieves significance only in the nonrecursive model, where it takes the largest standardized coefficient. The change in the power attributed to the effect of labor force participation on fertility is a function largely of the model used. In the recursive model the reciprocal effect of fertility in depressing black labor force participation was ignored, with the result that the effect of labor force participation on fertility was suppressed. The lack of large shifts in the parity measure comparable with the results among whites must partially be a function of the smaller effect this variable had on fertility in the black recursive model. The nonrecursive model increases both coefficients for the "program enrollment" variable.

From this analysis we conclude that "program enrollment," treated as an exogenous variable in recursive models, will continue to have similar effects in the same direction on dependent variables when put into nonrecursive models. Because the 1969 patient variable is exogenous, estimation of program effects in recursive models should not be biased.* Use of the unstandardized program enrollment coefficients to estimate program effects derived from less elaborate recursive models appears reasonable.†

The "Ecological Fallacy" and Interpretation of Areal Effects

The "ecological fallacy" is inherent in analysis of areal data.[7] If, for example, a negative relationship exists across areas between school enrollment and fertility, who is having fewer children and accounting for the negative relationship—women enrolled in school in areas of high enrollment, or women not enrolled in school in such areas—is unknown. The ecological fallacy is sidestepped by saying, in the above example, "Areas with high school enrollments have lower fertility than areas with low school enrollments." Similarly, a negative relationship between fertility and the proportion of women in need

---

*If a program reduced teen-age marriage, the program enrollment variable might be endogenous in analysis of SAU differences in the proportion never married at ages 15–19. By the same reasoning the program variable could be viewed as a cause of higher school enrollment, and hence endogenous in analysis of school enrollment rates. Given the low level of program development in 1969, the likelihood that the program variable actually assumed a powerful endogenous role for women 15–19 or older in 1969 seems remote. This does not imply that increased program impact on unwanted teen-age fertility could not result in program enrollment becoming an important endogenous variable in subsequent years.

†Most previous work using counties, states, or Standard Metropolitan Statistical Areas (SMSAs) as the areal unit of analysis ignore the problem of reciprocal effects. For a review of the U.S. literature, see J. DeFronzo, "Areal Analyses of Economic Factors Affecting the Birth Rate of Young Women: The United States, 1950–1970" (Ph.D. dissertation, Indiana University, 1975). For recursive analysis of county data, see D. M. Heer and J. W. Boyerton, "A multivariate regression analysis of differences in fertility of United States counties," *Social Biology*, 17 (3): 180–94, 1970. For recursive analysis of SMSAs see G. Cain and A. Weininger, "Economic determinants of fertility: results from cross-sectional aggregate data," *Demography*, 10:203–21, May 1973. A critique of the recursive models used in previous works using areal data is developed in DeFronzo, op. cit., along with nonrecursive models using state-level data.

who are patients in a family planning program does not provide absolute evidence that the lower fertility rate in areas with a high proportion of patients is actually a result of lower fertility among patients. Nonetheless, with adequate statistical controls on nonprogram factors related to fertility, testing for likely program effects net of other factors should be possible.

If the data form a pattern logically indicating such effects, the effects should exist because patients have lower fertility than they would have had in the absence of the program. This assumption would be undercut if a rationale could be developed explaining how the program effect depressing fertility occurs without the fertility of patients being affected. In the absence of such a rationale, we will assume that when areal analyses show program effects on fertility, such effects exist because patients have lower fertility than they would have had in the absence of a program.

Adjustment of Unstandardized Regression Coefficients Measuring Program Effects

Coefficients measuring program effects in our equations had to be adjusted to account for the disparity in timing between our count of patients and the fertility measure used as the dependent variable. Because county-level data on the number of patients in organized family planning programs for calendar year 1969 were considered more reliable than estimates for fiscal year 1968, the 1969 data were used. This is not the correct patient statistic to use in estimating program effects of children under one year at the time of the 1970 census (April 15, 1970). For a patient to avert a birth between April 16, 1969, and April 15, 1970, she would have had to enter the program between July 16, 1968, and July 15, 1969. The midpoint of this interval is January 15, 1969. Therefore, the correct count of patients in measuring program activity should be fitted to January 15, 1969.

From Table 1.1 estimates of patients as of June 30, 1967, June 30, 1968, and June 30, 1969, were plotted and the intercept in the 1968–69 fiscal year trend for January 15, 1969, was determined. This provided an estimate of 995,000 patients in the program at that time.

The calendar year 1969 patient count used in our SAU analysis was 1,201,329; when this number is divided by 995,000, a ratio of 1.207 results. This figure provides a multiplier used to adjust any unstandardized program enrollment regression coefficient related to measures of fertility.*

---

*Standardized regression coefficients, significance levels, and R^2 are not affected. All means and standard deviations in the text for program enrollment are for calendar 1969. Multiplying the calendar year 1969 program enrollment mean by .8285 (the reciprocal of 1.207) will yield the estimate for January 15, 1969. See Cutright and Jaffe, *op. cit.*, 1975, sec. 2.6.7, for mathematical justification of this adjustment procedure.

NOTES

1. These data are reported in Office of Economic Opportunity, *Need for Subsidized Family Planning Services: United States, Each State and County, 1969* (Washington, D.C.: U.S. Government Printing Office, 1972).

2. Center for Family Planning Program Development, *Need for Subsidized Family Planning Services: United States, Each State and County, 1971* (New York: Center for Family Planning Program Developments, 1973).

3. Obtained for Center for Family Planning Development Center, op. cit., 1973.

4. The procedure is described in detail in J. G. Dryfoos, "A formula for the 1970s: estimating need for subsidized Family Planning service in the United States," *Family Planning Perspectives*, 5:145–74, Summer 1973.

5. For a discussion of these issues, see P. Cutright and F. S. Jaffe, *Determinants and Demographic Impact of Organized Family Planning Programs in the U.S., 1969–1970* (New York: Alan Guttmacher Institute, 1975) chapter 2. An additional bias, tending to deflate our program effect coefficients for women below 200 percent of poverty, derives from the fact that 10 to 15 percent of patients in 1969 had incomes above this cutoff.

6. K. Schuessler, "Analyses of ratio variables: opportunities and pitfalls," *American Journal of Sociology*, 80:379–96, September 1974.

7. W. S. Robinson, "Ecological correlations and the behavior of individuals," *American Sociological Review*, 15:351–57, June 1950.

3

**DETERMINANTS OF
PROGRAM ENROLLMENT,
1969 AND 1971**

THEORETICAL AND MEASUREMENT ISSUES

A logically and temporally prior issue to program effects on fertility is the extent of program development in each area, measured by the proportion of women in need served by family planning programs. Areas differ on this basic measure of program enrollment. What are the determinants of this variation? We expect the extent to which women are enrolled as patients to depend on demographic characteristics, socioeconomic conditions, the health care delivery system, and family planning program activity in each SAU. We measure the effects of these variables on family planning program caseloads in calendar 1969 and fiscal 1971, using data from the 1970 census and from the Alan Guttmacher Institute.[1] This elaborates work by Daniel Weintraub and Bettie Nelson on the correlations between program activity characteristics and the proportion of need served that did not include controls for demographic and socioeconomic variables.[2]

Two measures of program enrollment are used. The preferred measure is the number of family planning patients with family incomes below 200 percent of poverty per 1,000 women in need, labeled PAT200/N.* This measure is

---

*Patient counts by county were reported for all women and for women with incomes below 150 percent of poverty in Center for Family Planning Program Development, 1973, op. cit. Table 1, p. 48. Cumulative rates for women below 150 percent of poverty and below 200 percent of poverty tabulated for 10 geographical regions were used to inflate patient counts to include an estimate of the number of patients between 151 percent and 200 percent of poverty, since our estimate of women in need covers those below 200 percent of poverty who are sexually active, fecund, and neither pregnant nor trying to become pregnant. See ibid., Table 12, p. 200.

This chapter was prepared by Michael Hout, assistant professor of sociology, University of Arizona, while a graduate student in the department of sociology at Indiana University.

preferred because both numerator and denominator include only those women with family incomes below 200 percent of poverty. Our data contained such poverty-specific patient counts for 1971 only. For 1969 we used the number of patients of all income levels per 1,000 women in need to estimate program success; this is of course the program enrollment variable used to estimate the impact of the 1969 program on fertility in subsequent chapters. Since almost all patients have incomes below twice the poverty level, this is not a major source of measurement error. In all comparisons between 1969 and 1971, we shall use program enrollment as the dependent variable for each year. Counts of patients by type of provider agency (hospital, health department, Planned Parenthood, or other) also were available for fiscal 1971,[3] and agency-specific patient ratios (for instance, hospital patients per 1,000 women in need) were computed.

The primary data for measuring program activity are counts in each county or SAU of the number of different agencies directly or indirectly providing family planning services (agencies); the number (from zero to four) of types of agencies providing family planning services (agentypes); and the number of unduplicated clinic locations (locations).[4] Agencies were available for fiscal 1971 only; agentypes and locations were available for both years. Using these primary data, we constructed three ratios: agencies per county, agentypes per county, and locations per 1,000 women in need. The two agency-related counts were divided by the number of counties in the SAU to standardize them to our unit of analysis. They are measures of the diversity of the family planning delivery system in the SAU, while accessibility of the services is indexed by locations per 1,000 women in need.

The demographic characteristics relevant to this analysis are the proportion of women living in rural areas (rural), the density of the population in the area to be served (log density), the proportion of women in prime childbearing years (age 20–29), and the racial composition of the area (white). Socioeconomic conditions include the economic need and social activity of women in the area. Since the target population for federally funded family planning programs is low-income and marginal-income women, we use three indicators of economic need: low education, public assistance, and low income. The indicators of social activity are "never married," "labor force," and "in school" (see Table 2.4).

Two aspects of the health care delivery system of an area affect a program's success in enrolling a large proportion of the population in need. The first is the accessibility of health care resources, indexed in our analyses by the number of primary-care physicians (including osteopaths) per 1,000 women in 1970 (doctors). The second is the extent to which health agencies that provide general health care to poor people also provide family planning services. This is indexed by the number of outpatient visits to hospitals providing family planning services per 1,000 outpatient visits to all hospitals (visits). Since low-income women utilize hospital outpatient departments to a greater degree than those with higher incomes, a high proportion of an area's outpatient visits in hospitals with family planning services means that the health care institutions in the SAU that are most in contact with low-income women for other types of health care also provide family planning services. Another index of the place of family planning services in the health care delivery system is the number of births in hospitals with family planning per 1,000 hospital births (births). Although we carried out most of the analysis using both visits and births, these variables are highly correlated (.91 in 1969 and .96 in 1971) and the results are redundant. A separate analysis of births is therefore omitted.

DETERMINANTS OF ENROLLMENT OF PATIENTS BELOW 200 PERCENT OF POVERTY

In this section we estimate the impact of family planning program activity on enrollment of patients with family incomes below 200 percent of poverty in 1971. Ordinary least-squares regression methods provide unbiased and efficient estimates of the parameters of this type of model under certain assumptions.[5] For example, the predictions generated by the model are assumed to have a constant error variance—that is, the margin of error in making the predictions is constant over the whole range of prediction. That assumption is untenable in this analysis because SAUs having no agencies or locations also have no patients, but program enrollment and PAT200/N vary over an increasingly wide range as agencies and locations increase. Nonconstant error variance is called heteroscedasticity, and the preferred method to adjust for it is generalized least-squares. Such estimates can be obtained by several methods; we use the one proposed by H. Glejser.[6] The results will be presented without technical discussion; interested readers are referred to a multivariate statistics text.[7] The substantive meanings attached to ordinary and generalized least-squares coefficients are the same.

The results of the generalized least-squares regression analysis of patients below 200 percent of poverty per 1,000 women in need are presented in Table 3.1. Two forms of the basic model are presented. They differ in the variables used to measure agencies, one using the number of agencies providing family planning services, and the other the number of agency types, in the numerator. The unstandardized coefficients are in the first two columns and the standardized coefficients are in the last two.

The levels of explained variance (R^2) in the bottom row show that both forms of the model explain about two-thirds of the variance and fit the data quite well, with the agentypes form explaining an additional 2 percent. Issues of statistical significance aside, the substantive importance of a 2 percent difference by itself is minimal.

TABLE 3.1

Determinants of Number of Patients Below 200 Percent of Poverty
per 1,000 Women in Need by Measure of Agencies: Fiscal 1971

Independent Variable	Unstandardized Coefficient		Standardized Coefficient	
	Number of Agencies Form	Agentypes Form	Number of Agencies Form	Agentypes Form
Agencies/C	16.34*	n.i.	.32*	n.i.
Agentypes/C	n.i.	56.04*	n.i.	.50*
Locations/N	96.75*	74.99*	.30*	.23*
Rural	−.09*	−.03*	−.16*	−.05*
Log density	1.69	−.77	.05	−.02
Age 20-29	.42*	.20*	.10*	.05*
White	−.10	−.16*	−.08	−.13*
Never married	−.05	.04	−.01	.01
In school	.16	−.02	.03	−.00
Labor force	.10	.04	.04	.02
Public assistance	.22*	.08	.10*	.02
Low education	.18	.19*	.06	.06*
Low income	.14*	.09*	.12*	.08*
Doctors	5.29*	1.42	.07*	.02
Visits	.05*	.04*	.13*	.10*
Constant	−124.42	58.62	n.r.	n.r.
R^2	.64	.66	.64	.66

*Coefficient greater than twice its standard error−that is, significant at the .05 level.
Note: Generalized least-squares regressions.
n.i. = not included in equation.
n.r. = not relevant.
Source: FPP Impact Study.

The program activity variables are significantly related to PAT200/N in both forms of the model, while rurality, age structure, race, public assistance, education, income, and the health care variables achieve significance in one form or the other. The most important finding of the regression is shown in the standardized coefficients. Regardless of the form of the model, the program activity variables are the strongest determinants of PAT200/N, net of all other factors. In the number-of-agencies form the coefficients of the number of agencies and clinic locations are twice as large as those of rurality and three times as large as those of age structure, public assistance, and low income. In the agentypes form, the number of types of provider agencies takes a coefficient four times as large as the strongest nonprogram variable (race), while the number of clinic locations has a coefficient nearly twice as large. Thus program activity, not sociodemographic contextual factors, clearly accounts for most of the variance in the proportion of women in need served. If our analysis of program effects on fertility in later chapters shows that higher levels of program enrollment lead to lower fertility, then the findings of this analysis demonstrate the ways in which higher levels of program enrollment can be achieved: the higher the level of program activity, the higher the proportion of women in need served by the program.

The two forms of the model make possible an examination of the mechanisms through which increased program activity brings about increased program enrollment. Are all program activity variables—agencies, agentypes, and clinic locations—equally important in increasing program enrollment? What mix of number of provider agencies, types of provider agencies, and clinic locations is necessary to achieve a given proportion of women in need served? In the next section we examine these issues, based on the results presented in Table 3.1.

The Number-of-Agencies Form of the Model

The number-of-agencies form of the model posits that the type of provider agency is less important than the number in determining the proportion of women in need who enroll in family planning clinics. Implicit in the use of agencies/C as an independent variable is the hypothesis that the addition of every family planning agency per county to an SAU has the same effect on the proportion served regardless of the type of family planning facilities already available. Under the assumption that this hypothesis is true, from the first column of Table 3.1 we estimate that the addition of a single agency per county produces an increase of 16.34 patients below the poverty cutoff per 1,000 women in need. The addition of one location per 1,000 women in need increases the proportion served by 96.75 patients below the poverty cutoff per 1,000 women in need. Since the initiation of a new agency implies the opening of at least one new location, the two effects are best viewed together. A general formula for estimating the impact of adding j new agencies per county with k new locations per 1,000 women in need in 1971 is

$$\Delta PAT200/N = j16.34 + k96.75 \tag{3.1}$$

where $j \geq O$ and $k > 0$.

The values of j and k need not be confined to the set of positive integers. For example, if an SAU has one county and 8,000 women in need, the addition of one new agency with two locations yields $j = 1$ and $k = .25$* and a predicted increase of

$$\Delta PAT200/N = 16.34 + (.25)(96.75)$$

$= 40.53$ additional patients below the poverty cutoff per 1,000 women in need. Since this hypothetical SAU has 8,000 women in need, we predict an increase of $8 \times 40.53 = 324.22$ patients. Equation 3.1 can be applied to situations where the desired change entails only the addition of locations to existing agencies by setting $j = 0$.

Weintraub and Nelson make a number of policy recommendations in terms of the number of agencies, agentypes, and/or locations required to enable programs to serve at least 500 patients per 1,000 women in need.[8] Equation 3.1 can be used to make similar calculations for SAUs by setting $\Delta PAT200/N$ equal to the difference between the goal of $PAT200/N = 500$ and the observed $PAT200/N$ and then solving for j and k. Consider the case where the desired outcome is to raise the national average to 500 patients per 1,000 women in need. Although the interpretation of these calculations differs from the interpretation of calculations for a single SAU, the mathematics is the same. The average number of patients below the poverty cutoff per 1,000 women in need in 1971 was 129.53 per SAU.† The desired increase in patients served per 1,000 in need is $500 - 129.53 = 370.47$. Many combinations of agencies and/or locations could achieve this result. To obtain unique solutions, the value of j or k would have to be set. For example, if for some reason (such as cost) increasing the average number of agencies by only one per county were desirable, then k, the number of additional locations per 1,000 women in need required to reach the goal of 500 patients per 1,000 women in need, can be obtained:

$$370.47 = (1)(16.34) + k96.75$$
$$3.66 = k$$

Thus, an increase of one provider agency per county and 3.66 locations per 1,000 women in need would be required to reach the goal of 500 patients per

---

*k is locations per 1,000 women in need; this SAU has 2 locations and 8,000 women in need; therefore, $k = 2/8 = .25$.

†This differs from total U.S. patients per 1,000 women in need because we have eliminated women with incomes above 200 percent of poverty from the numerator and because SAUs have differences in the number of women in need. Assigning a weight to each SAU that is proportional to the number of women in need eliminates the difference between SAU statistics and national statistics; but if weights were used, equation 3.1 would have to be modified to accommodate the weighting. Modifications were made, but the differences between the results of the weighted and unweighted calculations were small; therefore we present only the unweighted calculations.

1,000 women in need. An across-the-board increase of 3.66 locations would not be required, only an average increase of 3.66.

For policy reasons, increasing only the number of locations and not the number of agencies might be desirable. Under these conditions we set $j = 0$:

$$370.47 = (0)(16.34) + k96.75$$
$$3.83 = k$$

Thus, with no increase in agencies, the goal of 500 patients per 1,000 women in need could be reached if there were an average increase of 3.83 locations per 1,000 women in need.

When $\Delta PAT200/N$ is fixed, there is a linear, negative relationship between j and k. If $\Delta PAT200/N$ is fixed at 370.47, the difference between 500 patients per 1,000 women in need and the 1971 mean, and k is set, then

$$370.47 = j16.34 + k96.75$$
$$j16.34 = 370.47 - k96.97$$
$$j = 22.67 - 5.92k$$

And if j is set, then

$$k = 3.83 - .17j$$

The Agentypes Form of the Model

The agentypes form of the model posits that diversity of agencies providing family planning services is more important than quantity in attracting patients. The hypothesis implicit in the use of agentypes/C is that the impact of adding a new agency with k locations of a type already providing services in that county (not SAU) on the proportion of women in need who are served does not differ from the impact of adding k new locations to the existing agency of that type. Under the assumption that this hypothesis is true, the coefficients in the second column of Table 3.1 imply that the general formula for the addition of i new agentypes per county and k new locations per 1,000 women in need is

$$\Delta PAT200/N = i56.04 + k74.99 \tag{3.2}$$

where $0 \leq i \leq 4$ and $k > 0$.

Returning to the hypothetical SAU with one county and 8,000 women in need, the addition of one agency of a new type with two locations per 1,000 women in need yields $i = 1$ and $k = .25$ and a predicted increase of

$$\Delta PAT200/N = 56.04 + (.25)(74.99)$$

= 74.79 additional patients below the poverty cutoff per 1,000 women in need. Since this hypothetical SAU has 8,000 women in need, we predict an increase of 8 × 74.79 = 598.30 patients. If the new agency with two locations is not of a new type, then $i = 0$ and $k = .25$, for a predicted increase of

$$\Delta PAT200/N = (0)(56.04) + (.25)(74.99)$$

= 18.75 patients per 1,000 women in need, and the predicted increase in the number of patients is 150.

The equation also enables us to estimate the increases in agency types and locations necessary to increase the proportion served to 500 patients below the poverty cutoff per 1,000 women in need. As shown above, this would have required an increase of 370.47 patients per 1,000 women in need in 1971. Setting PAT200/N = 370.47 and solving equation 3.2 alternately for i and k yields

$$i = 6.61 - 1.34k$$
$$k = 4.94 - .75i$$

Comparison of the Two Forms

The predictions of the two forms of this basic model are disparate, yet their fit (R^2) to the observed data is nearly indistinguishable. This apparent paradox can be partially resolved with more calculations based on the hypothetical SAU with one county and 8,000 women in need. The number-of-agencies form of the model predicted an increase of 40.53 patients below the poverty cutoff per 1,000 women in need by the addition of one agency with two locations, while the agentypes form predicted an increase of 74.79 patients per 1,000 women in need if the additional agency was a new type and 18.75 if it was not.

Changing perspective from a single increment to a series of increments in all SAUs with one county and 8,000 women in need, the proportion (p) of these increments that would have to involve new agentypes in order to generate the same predictions from both forms of the model can be calculated:

$$40.53 = 74.79(p) + 18.75(1 - p)$$
$$40.53 = (74.79 - 18.75)p + 18.75$$
$$21.78 = 56.04p$$
$$.3886 = p$$

This result means that if all changes involve the addition of one agency per county and if roughly 39 percent of all added agencies are new provider agentypes, then the two models will generate identical predictions in the aggregate. The differences remain important for individual program decisions; but taking all decisions together, there are conditions under which these differences cancel out, yielding the same predictions for both forms of the model at the aggregate level.

These calculations have assumed that every change involves one agency, an assumption that has enabled us to calculate p exactly. Actually the only way that values for p can be obtained is by setting equations 3.1 and 3.2 equal to each other. This yields one equation with three unknowns: i, j, and k. The number of agentypes is also constrained to be less than or equal to the number of agencies ($i \leq j$). This system of one equation, one inequality, and three unknowns theoretically has an infinite number of solutions; and, given the practical limits to the number of agencies and locations, it still has a very large number of feasible solutions. A general formula for p does not exist. The purpose of these calculations has not been to discover general formulas, but to illustrate how two forms of the same model can yield radically different predictions for individual SAUs and still have the same fit to the data for all SAUs.

No firm conclusion can be drawn from this comparison of the two models. Our calculations show that they make different predictions for individual cases, but summing over all cases yields practically the same amount of error. This result arises whenever the combination of new and old agentypes attains certain equilibrium values, and these values have been shown for hypothetical single-county SAUs with 8,000 women in need. This is the limit of the data at hand. Applying formulas 3.1 and 3.2 to observed changes since the end of fiscal 1971 is one way to test the two forms of the model. This procedure, however, has two limitations. First, neither form of the model has a time parameter; therefore, the appropriate lag between initiating a change in program activity and observing the expected change in the number of patients or in the proportion served is unspecified. Second, if the time lag is rather long, one or more of the demographic, socioeconomic, and health care variables may change; and formulas 3.1 and 3.2 assume that they are constant.* Another possibility would be to include both the number of agencies per county and

---

*Adaptation of the formulas to cope with this second problem is straightforward. Multiply each change in an independent variable by the appropriate unstandardized coefficient in Table 3.1 and add that product to equation 3.1 or 3.2. For example, if family incomes in the SAU increased so that the proportion of women in families with incomes below 50 percent of the U.S. median declined by 50 women per 1,000, then you would subtract $50 \times .14 = 7$ from equation 3.1 and $50 \times .09 = 4.5$ from equation 3.2.

the number of agentypes per county in the same equation. However, they are highly correlated ($r = .744$); and when such highly correlated variables are entered in the same equation, the estimates of their unique effects have very large sampling errors. Therefore, we made no calculations using both variables in the same equation.

Our inability to reach a firm conclusion on the relative merits of the two forms of the model should not obscure the very clear indication from these data that program activity is the most important determinant of patient enrollment. The standardized coefficients for the program structural variables in the third and fourth columns of Table 3.1 are much larger than any of the other coefficients. Regardless of the precise mechanism by which increases in number and types of provider agencies, or of clinic locations, raise the proportion of women in need served, the program's structure per se—and not contextual factors—accounts for most of the variance in the proportion of women in need served.

There are two interesting differences between the standardized coefficients for the two forms of the model. Estimates in column 3 of Table 3.1 for the number-of-agencies form indicate that agencies and locations are of equal importance in determining caseloads, but estimates for the agentypes form in column 4 indicate that agentypes are more important than locations. Also, the relative importance of the demographic, socioeconomic, and health care variables is greater in the number-of-agencies form. In the fourth column only one standardized coefficient for those variables—"white"—is larger than the corresponding coefficient in the third column.

Utilizing methods introduced by O. D. Duncan in 1966 and formalized by D. F. Alwin and R. M. Hauser,[9] we partitioned the direct and indirect effects of the demographic, socioeconomic, and health care variables. These computations[10] show that almost all the impact of density (78 percent) is mediated by socioeconomic conditions, and 55 percent of the total effect of racial composition is transmitted by the socioeconomic variables. Health care mediates between one-fourth and one-third of the total effects of the other two demographic variables and of low education and public assistance. The program activity variables account for one-third or more of the effects of public assistance, low education, and the health care variables, and one-fourth of the age composition variable.

In this section the determinants of the number of patients below the poverty cutoff per 1,000 women in need were examined, using data for fiscal 1971. The most important determinant of the proportion of women in need served is program activity, measured by the number and types of provider agencies and the number of clinic locations. This conclusion was reached by using two forms of a basic model. One stressed the importance of the quantity of program services supplied, as indicated by the number of provider agencies per county; the other stressed the importance of program diversity, as indicated by the number of provider agentypes (hospital, health department, Planned Parenthood, or other) per county. Both forms included a measure of the number of clinic locations per 1,000 women in need. Although the two forms of our model generated different predictions for individual cases, the error variance over all cases was only 2 percent larger for the number-of-agencies form than for the agentypes form. Our calculations failed to reject either form, and we suggested that their relative merits may be evaluated on the basis of their ability to forecast patient enrollments.

In other analyses we also examined the role of program activity as an intervening variable. Despite significant demographic and socioeconomic effects on the proportions of women in need served, a large part of these effects was attributed to the mediating influence of health care and program variables.

DETERMINANTS OF PROGRAM ENROLLMENT, 1969 AND 1971

In this section we assess changes between 1969 and 1971 in the determinants of program enrollment. We employ the same research strategy used above and begin with an explication of the basic model for each year. This will be followed by a comparison of the results for 1969 and 1971.

The preferred dependent variable for the 1969 and 1971 comparison is the number of patients below 200 percent of poverty per 1,000 women in need. But, as noted above, our data on patients served in 1969 include some who had incomes above 200 percent of poverty. Therefore, the dependent variable for both years in this section is the total number of patients served in organized programs per 1,000 women in need. This is the program enrollment variable that will be used to test for program effects on fertility in subsequent analyses. Data limitations also restrict attention to the agentypes form of the model.

Examining the standardized coefficients in Table 3.2, we see that the independent variables used in these equations explain 61 percent of the variation in program enrollment in 1969 and 67 percent in 1971. In both years the variables that are significantly related to program enrollment include agentypes, locations, rurality, race, and the health care variables; in 1971 age structure, public assistance, and low income also are significant. However, the strongest coefficients are those of the program activity variables: in both years the number of provider agentypes per county is four times greater than the most powerful nonprogram variable (race), and the number of clinic locations is 1.5 times greater in 1969 and 2.5 times greater in 1971. These equations demonstrate again that program activity is the principal determinant of program enrollment; the sociodemographic context is of secondary importance.

The unstandardized generalized least-squares coefficients of the agentypes form of our model for 1969 are presented in the first column of Table 3.2. Only

TABLE 3.2

Determinants of Program Enrollment: 1969 and 1971

Independent Variable	Unstandardized Coefficient		Standardized Coefficient	
	CY 1969	FY 1971	CY 1969	FY 1971
Agentypes/C	55.95*	52.09*	.46*	.41*
Locations/N	48.36*	98.24*	.15*	.27*
Rural	−.04*	−.05*	−.09*	−.08*
Log density	−.56	−.67	−.02	−.02
Age 20-29	−.03	.46*	−.01	.10*
White	−.11*	−.15*	−.11*	−.11*
Never married	.17	.22	.06	.05
In school	.02	−.10	.01	−.02
Labor force	.06	.03	.03	.01
Public assistance	−.01	.28*	−.00	.07*
Low education	.02	.15	.01	.04
Low income	.03	.11*	.03	.09*
Doctors	3.31*	4.83*	.05*	.06*
Visits	.03*	.04*	.08*	.09*
Constant	50.93	−80.18	n.r.	n.r.
R^2	.61	.67	.61	.67

CY = calendar year.

FY = fiscal year.

*Coefficient greater than twice its standard error.

Note: Generalized least-squares regressions.

n.r. = not relevant.

Source: FPP Impact Study.

six variables have significant effects: rural-urban and racial composition, two health care variables, and the two program activity variables.

Under the assumptions of the agentypes model, the results in the first column of Table 3.2 imply the following general formula for the addition of i new agentypes per county and k new locations per 1,000 women in need:

$$\text{program enrollment} = i55.95 + k48.36 \tag{3.3}$$

where $0 \leq i \leq 4$ and $k > 0$. Returning to our example of a hypothetical SAU with one county and 8,000 women in need, the addition of one agency of a new type with two locations yields $i = 1$ and $k = .25$, for a predicted increase of

$$\text{program enrollment} = 55.95 + (.25)(48.36)$$

= 68.04 patients per 1,000 women in need, and a predicted increase of 544.32 patients.

If the new agency with two locations is not of a new type, then $i = 0$ and $k = .25$, for a prediction of

program enrollment $= (0)(55.95) + (.25)(48.36)$

= 12.09 patients per 1,000 women in need, yielding a predicted increase of 96.72 patients.

The unstandardized generalized least-squares coefficients for 1971 are presented in the second column of Table 3.2. Three demographic variables, two socioeconomic variables, both health care variables, and both program activity variables have significant effects.

Under the assumptions of the agentypes model, these results imply the following formula for the addition of i agentypes per county and k locations per 1,000 women in need:

$$\text{program enrollment} = i52.09 + k98.24 \tag{3.4}$$

where $0 \leq i \leq 4$ and $k > 0$. Once again using the example of an SAU with one county and 8,000 women in need, the addition of one agency of a new type with two locations yields $i = 1$, $k = .25$, and

program enrollment $= 52.09 + (.25)(98.24)$

= 76.65 patients per 1,000 women in need, or 613.2 patients. If the new agency is not of a new type, then $i = 0$, $k = .25$, and the model predicts

program enrollment $= (0)(52.09) + (.25)(98.24)$

= 24.56 patients per 1,000 women in need, or 196.48 patients.

The principal difference between the 1969 and 1971 results is that in the 18 months between the two study periods, the effect of the location variable (clinic utilization) doubled. In 1969 each location per 1,000 women in need added 48.36 patients; by fiscal 1971 each location added 98.24 patients. We regard locations/N as a measure of accessibility. These results suggest that as family planning programs develop and increasing proportions of women in need are served, clinic utilization increases and community differences in the proportion served become more dependent on differences in the accessibility of services.

The coefficient for the number of provider agentypes per county did not change significantly over the period in question. This suggests that the effect of diversity of the delivery system remains relatively constant, even while levels of program enrollment and the impact of accessibility are rising rapidly. Inferences regarding trend and constancy that are based on only two time points are inherently risky, and the temptation to overgeneralize these results must be resisted. (In the next section of this chapter, conditions will be placed on the generality of these conclusions.)

Another difference between 1969 and 1971 is the emergence of significant effects of age structure, public assistance rate, and family income on the percent served. Socioeconomic differentials were insignificant in 1969, but by 1971 SAUs with high proportions of women who were aged 20–29, received public assistance, or had low family incomes had significantly higher proportions of women in need enrolled in subsidized family planning programs. This may have been a result of federal policy to give priority in grant allocation to programs serving low-income patients and located in low-income neighborhoods.

In conclusion, the most significant differences between 1969 and 1971 in the determinants of the proportion of women in need served by organized family planning programs was in the impact of clinic locations on patients. In 1969 each location per 1,000 women in need added approximately 48 patients per 1,000; in fiscal 1971 that value had increased to 98 patients. The effect of the number of provider agentypes was unchanged between 1969 and 1971. In both years these variables measuring program activity were the most important determinants of patient enrollment, outstripping demographic, socioeconomic, and health care factors in accounting for the variance in the proportion served.

DIFFERENCES IN THE DETERMINANTS OF THE PROPORTION SERVED BETWEEN SAUs WITH DIFFERENT NUMBERS OF WOMEN IN NEED

The analysis thus far has shown that program enrollment is primarily a function of program activity, as measured by the number and types of agencies, and the number of clinic locations, providing family planning services. We now explore whether these effects differ by population size. In this section SAUs are classified by the number of women in need of family planning services, a proxy measure of population size. Four categories yielded approximately equal numbers of SAUs: 219 SAUs with fewer than 5,000 women in need, 201 SAUs with 5,000 to 7,499 women in need, 170 SAUs with 7,500 to 11,999 women in need, and 189 SAUs with 12,000 or more women in need. This classification occurs for two reasons. Weintraub and Nelson[11] suggest that fewer agencies may be required to serve 500 patients per 1,000 women in need in counties with small numbers. Since the number of women in need is proportional to population size, this suggestion has programmatic importance because smaller areas tend to have fewer existing health care agencies that could serve as providers of family planning services; inducing a large number of agencies to become providers in such areas may not be feasible. We want to test this hypothesis for a universe that includes all communities, whether or not they have any patients and under controls for nonprogram factors affecting the proportion served. The second reason is to determine whether the observed increase in the impact of locations between 1969 and 1971 holds within categories of SAUs classified by size of need.

Weintraub and Nelson's hypothesis implies that the impact of agencies is greater in SAUs with smaller numbers of women in need than in SAUs with larger numbers. It also implies that the impact is great enough to overcome the very small proportions served in SAUs with low need. In terms of equations 3.1 and 3.2, Weintraub and Nelson's hypothesis is that smaller values of i and j are required to achieve 500 patients served per 1,000 women in need —that is, set $PAT200/N = 500$—in areas with smaller need than in areas with larger need.

Panel A of Table 3.3 presents the generalized least-squares coefficients necessary to calculate the values of j and k for each size of need category. Plugging the coefficients in rows 1 and 2 of Panel A into equation 3.1 yields

$$500 = j47.61 + k$$
95.23   for 0–4,999 women in need,
$$500 = j25.90 + k$$
56.57   for 5,000–7,499 women in need,
$$500 = j24.70 + k$$
82.05   for 7,500–11,999 women in need,
$$500 = j5.86 + k$$
136.03   for 12,000+ women in need.

Solving these equations for j yields

$j = 10.50 - 2.00k$ for 0–4,999 women in need,
$j = 19.31 - 2.17k$ for 5,000–7,499 women in need,
$j = 20.24 - 3.32k$ for 7,500–11,999 women in need,
$j = 85.32 - 23.21k$ for 12,000+ women in need.

These equations can be used to obtain the number of agencies per county required to achieve 500 patients per 1,000 women in need for any fixed number of locations per 1,000 women in need (k). Many of the solutions are unfeasible; for example, the equation for SAUs with 12,000+ women in need states that if an SAU has exactly one location per 1,000 women in need ($k = 1$), that SAU would have to have $85.32 - 23.21 = 62.11$ agencies per county.

TABLE 3.3

Effects of Number of Agencies and Locations on Two Measures of Program Enrollment, by Estimated Need in SAU and Measure of Agencies: 1969 and 1971

	Number of Women in Need			
Independent Variable	0–4,999 (219 SAUs)	5,000–7,499 (201 SAUs)	7,500–11,999 (170 SAUs)	12,000+ (189 SAUs)
A. Patients Below 200 Percent/N, 1971				
Agencies/C	47.61*	25.90*	24.70*	5.86*
Locations/N	95.23*	56.57*	82.05*	136.03*
R^2	.55	.57	.61	.62
Agentypes/C	56.40*	40.71*	36.78*	31.30*
Locations/N	94.52*	65.21*	84.00*	124.63*
R^2	.58	.60	.63	.63
Mean PAT200/N	65.07	96.20	140.42	229.87
Mean agencies/C	.68	1.04	1.44	3.87
Mean agentypes/C	.60	.79	1.01	1.89
Mean locations/N	.30	.44	.58	.56
B. Program Enrollment, 1969				
Agentypes/C	52.85*	46.81*	52.60*	42.46*
Locations/N	42.86*	42.17*	65.16*	102.58*
R^2	.47	.59	.58	.56
Mean program enrollment	33.17	49.61	86.39	167.55
Mean agentypes/C	.47	.67	.94	1.71
Mean locations/N	.18	.30	.42	.46
C. Program Enrollment, 1971				
Agentypes/C	62.12*	45.28*	41.51*	39.37*
Locations/N	110.50*	71.22*	94.76*	142.50*
R^2	.57	.59	.64	.66
Mean program enrollment	74.72	106.31	153.64	257.73
Mean agentypes/C	.60	.79	1.01	1.89
Mean locations/N	.30	.44	.58	.56

*Coefficient greater than twice its standard error.
Note: Generalized least squares regressions, unstandardized coefficients.
Source: FPP Impact Study.

To evaluate Weintraub and Nelson's hypothesis, we shall consider only those solutions that fall in the range between one and eight agencies per county. Three of the four means in the eighth row of Panel A fall in that range; the mean for SAUs with fewer than 5,000 women in need is less than one. Figure 3.1 contains graphs of the four equations. The segments between one and eight agencies per county are the feasible solutions.

Figure 3.1 provides conditional support for Weintraub and Nelson's hypothesis that fewer agencies are required to reach 500 patients per 1,000 women in SAUs with smaller numbers of women in need. In these SAUs, achieving 500 patients per 1,000 women with a feasible number of agencies per county and fewer than 1.25 locations per 1,000 women in need is impossible. But if the number of locations per 1,000 women in need is set at 1.25, programs in SAUs with fewer than 5,000 women in need can serve 500 per 1,000 women

FIGURE 3.1
Number of Agencies per County and Locations per 1,000 Women in Need Required to Achieve an Enrollment Rate of 500 Patients per 1,000 Women in Need, by Number of Women in Need per SAU: 1971

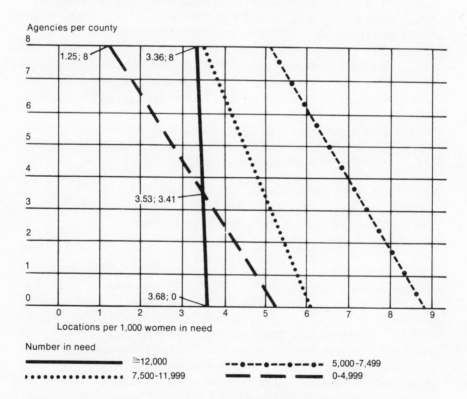

Agencies per county

Locations per 1,000 women in need

Number in need

─────────── ≧12,000   ──●──●──●──●── 5,000-7,499

●●●●●●●●●●●●●● 7,500-11,999   ─── ── ── ── 0-4,999

if they have eight agencies per county. For any number of locations between 1.25 and 3.53 per 1,000 women in need, low-need SAUs are the only ones that could serve 500 patients per 1,000 women in need with a feasible number of agencies per county. At 3.53 locations per 1,000 women in need, SAUs with 12,000$^+$ could also serve 500 patients per 1,000 in need with a feasible number of agencies per county; but for fewer than 3.53 locations per 1,000, low-need SAUs could achieve 500 patients per 1,000 with fewer agencies. If locations are set at 3.53 per 1,000, both low-need and high-need SAUs could achieve 500 patients per 1,000 with 3.41 agencies per county. With more than 3.53 locations per 1,000, high-need SAUs can achieve higher ratios of patients to need than low-need SAUs can.

Thus, serving 500 patients per 1,000 women in need appears to require at least 1.25 locations per 1,000 women in need; within the range of 1.25 to 3.53 locations per 1,000 women in need, the number of agencies per county required to attain this objective in SAUs with relatively small numbers of women in need seems feasible, and 1.25–3.53 is less than or equal to the number required in SAUs with larger numbers of women in need. For more than 3.53 locations per 1,000 women in need, low-need SAUs require more agencies per county than do high-need SAUs. This pattern results from the fact that the effect of a single agency per county is highest in low-need SAUs but the effect of a single location (that is, clinic utilization) is greatest in high-need SAUs.

When agentypes rather than agencies are considered, however, all minimum solutions are in the category of 12,000$^+$ women in need. Solving equation 3.2 for i using the coefficients in rows 4 and 5 of Panel A yields

$$i = 8.82 = 1.67k \quad \text{for 0–4,999 women in need,}$$
$$i = 12.37 - 1.61k \quad \text{for 5,000–7,499 women in need,}$$
$$i = 13.52 - 2.27k \quad \text{for 7,500–11,999 women in need,}$$
$$i = 16.04 - 4.00k \quad \text{for 12,000}^+ \text{ women in need.}$$

Since there are only four agentypes, the feasible range for solutions to these equations is $1 \leq i \leq 4$. The graphs of the equations are drawn in Figure 3.2.

Only in the range from 2.89 to 3.10 locations per 1,000 women in need is the number of agentypes required to reach 500 patients per 1,000 in low-need SAUs both feasible and less than the number required in high-need SAUs. As with numbers of agencies, the greatest impact of agentypes is in low-need SAUs; but the differences in the coefficients among the size-of-need categories are smaller. The curvilinear pattern of utilization is the same.

The mixed result for Weintraub and Nelson's hypothesis does not discount the importance of their observation that the impact of program activity depends on the size of the need in the area to be served. The differences are very important; and better predictions regarding the outcomes of changes in

FIGURE 3.2
Number of Agency Types per County and Locations per 1,000 Women in Need Required to Achieve an Enrollment Rate of 500 Patients per 1,000 Women in Need, by Number of Women in Need per SAU: 1971

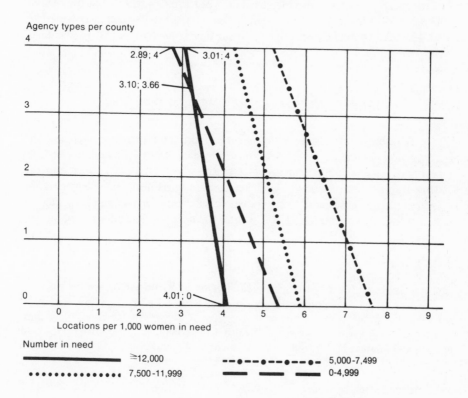

Agency types per county

Locations per 1,000 women in need

Number in need

━━━━━━ ≧12,000		━●━━●━━●━ 5,000-7,499
●●●●●●●●●●● 7,500-11,999		━━ ━━ ━━ 0-4,999

the number of agencies, agentypes, and locations can be achieved by taking size of need into account, using the coefficients in Table 3.3 rather than those in Table 3.1. The standard deviation of the errors of prediction for the number-of-agencies form of the model is 82.33 using the coefficients in Table 3.1 and 78.64 using those in rows 1 and 2 in Panel A of Table 3.3; the standard deviation of the errors for the agentypes form is 79.77 in Table 3.1 and 76.70 in rows 4 and 5 of Panel A of Table 3.3.

The second reason for classifying SAUs by size of need was to replicate the observation, made in the section of this chapter entitled "Determinants of Program Enrollment, 1969 and 1971," that the impact of locations on patients (that is, clinic utilization) increased between 1969 and 1971. Comparing the second row of Panel B in Table 3.3 with the second row of Panel C shows increases in the coefficients in all four size-of-need categories. The largest increase was in SAUs with the smallest need, where the number of patients per location nearly tripled between 1969 and 1971 from 42.86 per 1,000 in need to 110.50. In the SAUs with larger numbers of women in need, the coefficients of the location variable also increased between 1969 and 1971, but the relative increases declined as the size of need increased: the relative increases were 158, 69, 45, and 39 percent, respectively, for the lowest-need to highest-need categories.

DIFFERENCES AMONG PROVIDER AGENCIES

To assess differences in the effects of different provider agencies, the proportion of patients in each SAU served by each type of provider agency was regressed on the number of agencies of the given type per county and the demographic, socioeconomic, and health care variables. The coefficients for agencies from those regressions and the coefficients for a comparison regression using all patients per 1,000 women in need as dependent variable are presented in Table 3.4.

TABLE 3.4

Effects of Number of Specific Types of Provider Agencies on Program Enrollment: Fiscal 1971

Independent Variable	Hospital	Health Department	Planned Parenthood	Other Agencies	All Agencies
Hospitals/C	12.83*	n.i.	n.i.	n.i.	7.24*
Health department/C	n.i.	93.35*	n.i.	n.i.	42.07*
Planned parenthoods/C	n.i.	n.i.	118.54*	n.i.	73.09*
Other agencies/C	n.i.	n.i.	n.i.	27.79*	23.84*
Locations/N	n.i.	n.i.	n.i.	n.i.	96.16*
R^2	.42	.42	.43	.19	.67

*Coefficient greater than twice its standard error.
Note: Generalized least-squares regression, unstandardized coefficients.
        n.i. = not included in equations.
Source: FPP Impact Study.

The results are what would be expected on the basis of published reports of the proportions of the total caseload served by each type of agency.[12] The largest effect, 118.54 patients added per 1,000 women in need, is associated with an increase of one Planned Parenthood affiliate in an SAU. Adding a health department clinic yields an increase of 93.35 patients per 1,000 women in need. Other provider agencies and hospitals have smaller but still significant effects. Regressing patients served by all types of provider agencies per 1,000 women in need on the number of agencies by type produces the same rank order in the magnitude of effects. The R^2 of .67 in the last column is the same as the R^2 for the agentypes form of the basic model reported in Table 3.2.

SUMMARY

The most important direct determinant of the proportion of women in need served by U.S. family planning programs in 1969 and 1971 was program activity, measured by the number and types of agencies providing the services and the number of locations at which they were provided. Our basic causal model specified that the proportion served depends on demographic, socioeconomic, health care, and program activity variables. Two forms of the basic model, one stressing quantitative aspects of program structure and the other stressing diversity, were compared using 1971 data. Although the two forms of the model differ on individual cases, neither could be rejected when the error variance over all cases was used as the criterion for rejection.

Whichever model was employed, however, the coefficients related to these program variables invariably were considerably larger than those associated with any of the nonprogram variables measuring the demographic, socioeconomic, or health care contexts. The proportion of low-income and marginal-income women in need of family planning who are served by clinic programs thus varies primarily as a function of program effort and can be raised by increasing the number and types of provider agencies and the number of clinic locations. Compared with the demographic, socioeconomic, and health care factors, these program activity variables are modified relatively easily through the allocation of additional resources that can facilitate the formation of new agencies and induce existing provider agencies to offer services at additional clinic locations. The findings of this chapter thus form a crucial link between policy change and the programs' impact on fertility.

We also found an important change in the impact of these program activity variables between 1969 and 1971. The effect of the number of clinic locations on the proportion of women in need who are served increased dramatically. This increase was observed for all SAUs as well as in all categories of SAUs classified by the number of women in need. The number of provider agentypes per county had similar effects on the proportion served in both years for all SAUs as well as in SAUs grouped by size of need.

NOTES

1. Office of Economic Opportunity, *Need for Subsidized Family Planning Services: United States, Each State and County, 1969* (Washington, D.C.: U.S. Government Printing Office, 1972); and Center for Family Planning Program Development, *Need for Subsidized Family Planning Services: United States, Each State and County, 1971* (New York: Center for Family Planning Program Development, 1971).

2. D. R. Weintraub and B. L. Nelson, "Components of successful county family planning programs: a suggested model for program development" (New York: Center for Family Planning Program Development, 1974). (Unpublished.)

3. Center for Family Planning Program Development, 1973, op. cit., Table 1, p. 48.

4. Office of Economic Opportunity, 1969, op. cit., Table 1, p. 44; Center for Family Planning Program Development, 1973, loc. cit.

5. J. Johnston, *Econometric Methods* (2nd ed.; New York: McGraw-Hill, 1971), pp. 135–40.

6. Ibid., pp. 208–21; H. Glejser, "A new test for heteroscedasticity," *Journal of the American Statistical Association,* 64: 316–23, 1969.

7. For instance, Johnston, op. cit.

8. Weintraub and Nelson, op. cit.

9. O. D. Duncan, "Path analysis: sociological examples," *American Journal of Sociology,* 72:1–16, July 1966; D. F. Alwin and R. M. Hauser, "The decomposition of effects in path analysis," *American Sociological Review,* 40:37–47, February 1975.

10. For the detailed calculations see P. Cutright and F. S. Jaffe, *Determinants and Demographic Impact of Organized Family Planning Programs in the U.S., 1969–1970* (New York: Alan Guttmacher Institute, 1975) p. 71ff, ch. 3.

11. Weintraub and Nelson, op. cit., p. 7.

12. Center for Family Planning Program Development, op. cit.

4

MEASURING PROGRAM
EFFECTS ON
FERTILITY RATES

This chapter examines factors affecting different measures of fertility among SAUs throughout the nation. We seek to acquaint the reader with the structure of the data, the general pattern of relationships among variables, and the factors that help explain differences among SAUs in children ever born (CEB) per 1,000 white and black women aged 15-44. We supplement this with analysis of variables related to areal differences in childlessness and the number of children born in 1969 to women age 15-44, by race. These analyses lead to consideration of historic differences in family planning delivery systems between communities that can, if left uncontrolled, produce spurious estimates of 1969 program effects on 1969-70 fertility rates.

The validity of our view of these historic differences is tested with data for CEB to white and black wives, by age and poverty level. These tests allow confidence in the model used in chapters 5 and 6 to estimate family planning program effects on 1969-70 fertility.

ANALYSES OF VARIOUS FERTILITY RATES, BY RACE

Means per SAU and standard deviations of variables used in the following analyses of white and black women aged 15-44 are shown in Table 4.1. For example, among whites aged 15-44 in all marital and economic statuses, the mean CEB in all 778 SAUs was 1,733. The mean 1969 general fertility rate per SAU was 87 per 1,000 women, and 376 per 1,000 were childless. The mean number of women 15-44 who were aged 20-29 was 352 per 1,000. The measure of population density (space) does not change across age groups because it measures an SAU characteristic, not that of a subgroup of women. Similarly, the program enrollment variable measuring the number of patients per 1,000

TABLE 4.1

Means and Standard Deviations of Variables in Analyses of All Women Aged 15-44: 1970

Variable	White		Black	
	Mean	S.D.	Mean	S.D.
Program enrollment	82	111	142	113
CEB	1,733	180	2,194	225
1969 fertility rate	87	17	116	19
Childless rate	376	42	353	30
Age 20–29	352	34	338	30
Space	–4.73	1.56	–5.40	1.54
Low education	47	39	123	64
Migration	266	88	151	83
Never married	272	42	371	47
In school	197	31	218	34
Labor force	438	57	498	72
Number of SAUs	778		237	

Note: The SAU mean of parity 1969 can be derived from CEB and 1969 fertility and, therefore, is excluded.

Source: FPP Impact Study.

women in need does not change because it is not age-specific. Even in sub-groups where the number of SAUs varies,* the difference in the mean value of these two constant variables is so small that we generally do not report it.

The remaining statistics in the table show data for white and black women and are compatible with national data from other sources that also find that black women have higher levels of fertility and labor force participation, fewer years of schooling, and a smaller proportion ever married than white women do. We are less interested in racial differences than in the results of analysis of these data within racial groups, and we now report some parts of the analyses that helped form the model used in later chapters to estimate the effects of program enrollment on 1969–70 fertility. Since the purpose here is illustrative, we report only analyses of women aged 15-44, reserving age-specific analysis for later tables.

---

*SAUs with fewer than 300 women in a given subgroup are always omitted. The extent to which an analysis of a particular subgroup is representative of all SAUs in the nation can be judged by comparing the number of SAUs in a given subgroup analysis with the total count of 778 white or 237 black SAUs. Because SAUs with large populations suffer less attrition in subgroup analysis than do SAUs with smaller populations, the loss of, say, 25 percent of SAUs in a given equation would not mean that 25 percent of the national population was omitted. The actual loss would be something less than 25 percent.

Table 4.2 shows the results of regressions on four measures of fertility among white and black women aged 15-44 in all economic and marital statuses: (1) CEB, (2) parity in 1969, (3) the number of childless women per 1,000, and (4) the 1969 fertility rate. In column 4 the equations omit the independent variable measuring 1969 parity, while the equations in column 5 include the parity measure. The net effect of each independent variable on each fertility rate is measured by the unstandardized regression coefficient, which estimates the impact of a change of one unit of an independent variable on each fertility

TABLE 4.2

Effects of Independent Variables on Various Fertility Measures, All Women Aged 15–44, by Race: 1970

Independent Variable	CEB (1)	Parity 1969N (2)	Zero CEB (3)	1969 Fertility Rate	
				No Parity (4)	With Parity (5)
White					
Program enrollment	−.308*	−.295*	.034*	−.013	−.004
Age 20–29	−1.507*	−1.603*	.332*	.096*	.146*
Space	41.913*	39.737*	−4.011*	2.177*	.924
Low education	−.088	−.181	.044*	.093*	.098*
Migration	−.170*	−.178*	.076*	.008	.014
Never married	−.241	−.272*	.754*	.031	.039
In school	.078	.097	.105*	−.019	−.022
Labor force	−.807*	−.765*	.055*	−.042*	−.018
Parity 1969N	n.i.	n.i.	n.i.	n.i.	.032*
R^2	.66	.68	.92	.12	.15
Number of SAUs	778				
Black					
Program enrollment	−.256*	−.239*	.037*	−.017	−.001
Age 20–29	.072	−.112	−.104	.185*	.192*
Space	57.231*	53.563*	−3.602*	3.668*	.086
Low education	1.606*	1.542*	.060*	.064*	−.039
Migration	−.384*	−.390*	.057*	.006	.032
Never married	−1.591*	−1.497*	.409*	−.094*	.006
In school	.853*	.814*	.269*	.040	−.015
Labor force	−.411*	−.360*	.012	−.050*	−.026
Parity 1969N	n.i.	n.i.	n.i.	n.i.	.067*
R^2	.69	.70	.66	.22	.38
Number of SAUs	237				

*$p < .05$.

Note: Ordinary least-squares regressions, unstandardized coefficients.
    n.i. = not included in equations.
Source: FPP Impact Study.

measure, net of other factors in the same equation. We focus attention in this table on coefficients related to the program enrollment variable.

In the analysis of white CEB, R^2 is .66, indicating that the set of independent variables explains two-thirds of the variance in the dependent variable. The interpretation of the program enrollment coefficient would be that for every 100 patients served per 1,000 women estimated to be in need of services, there would be 30.8 fewer CEB per 1,000 white women aged 15-44. The second dependent variable (parity, 1969N) is the result of subtracting the 1969 general fertility rate from CEB. In this case R^2 is .68 and the program enrollment coefficient indicates a reduction of about 29.5 births for each 100 additional patients per 1,000 women in need. The difference between the coefficients in columns 1 and 2 will equal the program enrollment coefficient in analysis of 1969 general fertility rates, using the same predictors (column 4). In analysis of 1969 general fertility (omitting the parity measure), R^2 is only .12 and the program activity coefficient is -.013 (the difference between -.308 and -.295), and is not significant. The program coefficient is likewise insignificant when 1969 parity is included in the equation (column 5), but it is significantly and positively related to childlessness (column 3), where R^2 reaches .92.

Among black women 15-44, program enrollment has significant negative effects on CEB and 1969 parity, and is positively and significantly related to childlessness. It has no significant negative effect on 1969 general fertility rates when the parity measure is omitted (column 4), and loses significance and is almost wiped out when it is included (column 5). The levels of explained variance among blacks are similar to those for whites—quite high in analyses of CEB, 1969 parity, and childlessness and much lower in analyses of the 1969 general fertility rate.

The relationship of program enrollment to childlessness helps explain the negative relationship of the program variable to CEB and 1969 parity. Despite the strong relationship of the program to childlessness, the program coefficient is not significantly related to 1969 general fertility rates.

Can these negative and significant coefficients to CEB and 1969 parity, and positive and significant coefficients to childlessness, among white and black women in all socioeconomic and marital statuses be interpreted as evidence of an effect of the 1969 program? This seems implausible on its face. We cannot regard the program enrollment coefficient for cumulative measures of fertility as the result of there being few or many patients in organized family planning programs in 1969.

Both white and black women have significant program coefficients; these coefficients require explanation, particularly because of the degree of statistical control we have on other factors affecting fertility. We believe that a plausible explanation lies in antecedent factors that led to the presence or absence of a family planning clinic in an area in 1969—and, indeed, to its 1969 level of program enrollment. Although 1969 was an early point in the evolution of the overall national family planning program, in many communities clinics had been initiated decades before by affiliates of the Planned Parenthood Federation. These tended to be in the larger cities (which also have more hospitals, physicians, and other health resources). As a result the availability of family planning services in different communities was differentiated in two ways—directly, by the services provided by the Planned Parenthood clinics, and indirectly, by the effects of the organization's efforts on the attitudes and policies of other health institutions and professionals toward fertility control. (Moreover, the greater availability of health resources in cities with Planned Parenthood affiliates could partially account for a greater availability of family planning even if the Planned Parenthood organization had little or no indirect influence.) In fact, when federal funds for family planning services first became available in modest amounts (1965), cities with established family planning agencies and staffs were the first to obtain federal grants to expand their programs. By 1969, the year in which we measure program enrollment, many communities with the most advanced clinic programs were those in which the Planned Parenthood organization had functioned for a long time.

The program enrollment measure thus taps some historic differences between communities in the availability of family planning services—and this factor lends credence to the negative coefficients of this variable on pre-1969 fertility. Simply put, in communities where Planned Parenthood, hospitals, and physicians were more likely to have provided birth control services in the past, expansion of organized family planning programs was easier in the mid-1960s than in communities in which the health community had less experience with the provision of birth control services. Therefore, communities with a greater proportion of patients in 1969 tended to be those in which the health community was more likely to have provided birth control services in the past.

While clinic services were provided primarily to lower-income groups, the indirect effects could have influenced patterns of other groups and thus could have affected cumulative fertility rates in all groups in the community. If so, analysis of cumulative measures of fertility by poverty status should find negative patient coefficients to CEB among women both above and below the poverty status cutoff. This hypothesis is tested below.

In sum, negative program coefficients on cumulative measures of fertility do not arise from the fact that an area had few or many patients in 1968–69, and we do not propose these cumulative measures as preferred dependent variables with which to assess program impact. But they can arise from program-related factors that governed the timing and growth of organized programs in different types of communities. The effects of these historic factors are interesting and must be considered carefully.[1]

But systematic analysis of program effects on fertility caused by having a small or large proportion of women in need who are clinic patients cannot use cumulative measures and must rely, instead, on current fertility rates. For example, among whites and blacks the effects of program enrollment on 1969 general fertility rates is completely eliminated when 1969 parity is included in the regressions. As noted above, effects of clinic enrollment in years prior to 1969 could have been a cause of 1969 parity among whites and blacks aged 15-44; but our interest is in a clear-cut test of the effect of clinic enrollment in 1968–69 on 1969–70 fertility. Introducing parity is a valid method of controlling both for possible pre-1969 program effects and for other characteristics of areas that affect fertility but are not measured by our other independent variables.

The analyses in Table 4.2 do not reveal evidence of 1968–69 clinic enrollment effects on the 1969 general fertility rate. Using measures of annual fertility specific to the population subgroup from which the program's patients are drawn and controlling for fertility prior to the study year are necessary, however, to provide a genuine test of program effects. Analyses of annual subgroup fertility rates are presented in chapters 5 and 6. The remainder of this chapter examines the role of the program enrollment measure in analyses of children ever born to subgroups of white and black wives.

CHILDREN EVER BORN TO WIVES, BY RACE, AGE, AND POVERTY

We now analyze children ever born to wives living with their husbands in 1970, a measure of marital fertility specific to age, race, and poverty status. This is, of course, a cumulative fertility measure. By comparing the regression coefficients of the program variable for women in all economic statuses with the coefficients for women below and above the poverty cutoff, however, we can test whether the negative coefficients shown in the previous analyses emerge because of historic community differences depressing the fertility of only upper-income or lower-income women, with an additional control on marital status. This set of analyses is specific to wives aged 20-29 and 30-44, as well as the 15-44 age group, thus allowing further specification of variables that affect the number of children ever born to white and black wives.

Children Ever Born to White Wives

Table 4.3 displays means and standard deviations of the variables used in the analysis of fertility among white, spouse-present wives at all economic

TABLE 4.3

Means and Standard Deviations of Variables in Analyses of White Wives, by Age and Poverty Status: 1970

Age	Variable	All Wives		Below 200% Pov.		Above 200% Pov.	
		Mean	S.D.	Mean	S.D.	Mean	S.D.
15–44	CEB	2,386	269	3,082	384	2,077	222
	Children under one year	116	13	172	21	92	14
	Age 20–29	395	32	403	46	391	32
	Low education	43	43	81	69	23	18
	Migration	296	92	303	112	293	87
	Never married*	272	43	282	41	266	45
	In school	28	15	30	25	28	13
	Labor force	419	63	269	57	487	70
20–29	CEB	1,581	193	2,231	276	1,288	151
	Children under one year	202	23	272	37	171	26
	Low education	27	31	55	52	12	11
	Migration	412	110	399	125	418	106
	Never married*	182	65	186	85	179	64
	In school	37	25	37	39	37	21
	Labor force	402	73	250	65	473	81
30–44	CEB	3,070	325	4,018	376	2,683	283
	Children under one year	45	10	74	19	34	9
	Low education	54	53	105	88	30	25
	Migration	209	79	219	96	207	76
	Never married*	45	23	47	21	44	25
	Labor force	435	62	281	57	499	71

*Mean SAU value per 1,000 women never married in all marital statuses, a proxy for age at first marriage.

Note: Number of SAUs in all analyses is 778. See Table 4.1 for mean program enrollment and space per SAU.

Source: FPP Impact Study.

levels, and by poverty and age.* Comparisons across the rows finds expected differences between wives below and above the poverty cutoff, although little difference is found for several variables. Large differences occur in CEB as well

---

*Married, spouse-present women aged 15-19 are omitted from this section because only 8 percent of black and 11 percent of white teen-agers were living with husbands in 1970. The effect of program enrollment on the fertility of teen-age wives is examined in chapter 5.

as children under one year for wives 15-44 and for the two age subgroups. Another large and consistent difference is that in each age group the labor force participation rate among wives above 200 percent of poverty is almost twice the rate among those below it; no doubt this partially explains how they come to be above the poverty cutoff.

Because both smaller family size and higher labor force participation are causal factors determining whether a family is above the poverty cutoff, these differences are expected. Little difference, by poverty, occurs in the level of migration, age at first marriage (using the rate for all women in the subgroup "never married" as our indicator), school enrollment, or age composition. Although poorer women are more likely to have less education, the absolute difference between poverty groups is only 4 to 8 percent.

Table 4.4 displays the level of explained variance and unstandardized coefficients, by poverty, of independent variables regressed on children ever born to wives aged 15-44, 20-29, and 30-44. R^2 is quite high for all wives and those aged 20-29, but lower for older women. Among all wives aged 15-44, SAUs with high ratios of land per capita and with late age at marriage (that is, high proportions never married) tend to have larger CEBs. This unexpected effect of marital status generally disappears under age-specific analysis. School enrollment, labor force participation, migration, and program enrollment all have significant, negative coefficients. The program coefficient is negative and significant for all wives, an expected finding that may be the result of historic factors related to pre-1969 program development on fertility of wives. Neither age nor education takes a significant coefficient.

Among white wives aged 15-44 below the poverty cutoff, the pattern of effects generally is similar in sign to that found among all wives. All variables are significant. Age structure now has a significant negative relationship to CEB, and areas with higher proportions of wives with few years of schooling tend to have lower cumulative fertility than other areas do. This is an unexpected finding for which no apparent explanation is immediately available, unless areal differences in marital instability are positively related to low education and affect marital duration of currently married women. The program enrollment measure is negative and significant for wives below the poverty cutoff. Among white wives aged 15-44 above the poverty cutoff, only the coefficients for age structure and migration are not significant. All significant coefficients—including the program variable—take the same sign as in the group below the cutoff.

The center and right-hand panels of the table show coefficients for wives aged 20-29 and 30-44. Within each age group and in all three SES groups, the program enrollment measure has a significant negative relationship to CEB. In the older age group this effect is actually larger among wives above the poverty cutoff than among those below it. The remaining variables take their expected relationships to CEB and generally are significant. Nearly all coeffi-

TABLE 4.4

Effects on CEB per 1,000 White Wives, by Age and Poverty Status: 1970

Age and Poverty Status

Independent Variable	15-44			20-29			30-44		
	All Wives	<200% Poverty	>200% Poverty	All Wives	<200% Poverty	>200% Poverty	All Wives	<200% Poverty	>200% Poverty
Program enrollment	-.480*	-.612*	-.435*	-.252*	-.484*	-.245*	-.465*	-.422*	-.494*
Age 20-29	-.148	-2.230*	-.024	n.i.	n.i.	n.i.	n.i.	n.i.	n.i.
Space	87.122*	26.165*	48.311*	54.907*	13.907*	11.423*	100.861*	46.753*	37.744*
Low education	.040	-.623*	-2.641*	.535*	-.287*	-1.325*	-.359*	-.525*	-3.656*
Migration	-.181*	-.392*	.001	-.472*	-.623*	-.276*	-.968*	-.873*	-.591*
Never married	2.912*	2.683*	1.767*	.039	.525*	-.421*	.211	-.211	-.965*
In school	-4.797*	-4.915*	-2.469*	-2.080*	-3.570*	-1.402*	n.i.	n.i.	n.i.
Labor force	-1.162*	-1.433*	-1.119*	-.864*	-.949*	-.924*	-2.132*	-2.396*	-1.448*
R^2	.69	.65	.54	.75	.62	.51	.45	.23	.38

*$p < .05$.
Notes: Number of SAUs in all analyses = 778. Ordinary least-squares regressions, unstandardized coefficients.
n.i. = not included in equation.
Source: FPP Impact Study.

cients are negatively related to fertility. In contrast with the results for wives 15-44, the proportion never married, in age-specific analysis, takes negative coefficients in three of the four subsets. Only among younger wives below the poverty cutoff is this proxy for age at first marriage positively related to children ever born. This switching of signs is evidence of interaction effects that were not adequately controlled in the analysis of wives of all ages. It also suggests that program enrollment coefficients for age-specific groups have greater validity than similar coefficients for women of all ages.

Children Ever Born to Black Wives

The means and standard deviations for fertility rates and independent variables used in the analysis of children ever born to black wives are displayed in Table 4.5. Again we find large differences both in fertility measures and in labor force participation rates above and below the poverty cutoff. Differences in the proportion never married above and below the cutoff are greater among blacks than among whites. Higher-income black wives are somewhat more likely to have lived in a different county in 1965 than 1970 and to be enrolled in school, and are much less likely to have few years of schooling, than black wives below the poverty cutoff. Age composition of the two poverty status groups is similar.

Table 4.6 shows that among black wives aged 15-44 in all poverty statuses, only school enrollment and migration fail to take significant coefficients to CEB. Explained variance is .86, indicating a very high level of explanation of differences among areas in black CEB. Low education and space are positively related to fertility, as is the never-married measure. In areas with a high proportion of women never married, black wives aged 15-44 have a higher number of children ever born. (As with whites, this variable changes sign under age-specific analysis.) Program enrollment and labor force participation are negatively related to CEB among blacks, as was the case for whites. Program enrollment is negatively related both above and below the poverty cutoff.

With the exception of low education and migration, the coefficients take the same signs for wives aged 15-44 above and below the poverty cutoff. Migration and school enrollment are not significant in either group. In the higher-income group only age, the proportion married, and the program activity measure are significant. The low level of explained variance in CEB among higher-income black wives is in sharp contrast with that among low-income wives and wives in all poverty statuses. As noted in chapter 2, the recursive models in these analyses may be suppressing effects of independent variables like labor force participation that are, in part, a function of the level of fertility.

In the center and right-hand panels, explained variance is very high for ages 20-29 and 30-44 when all poverty levels are combined, but it is lower

TABLE 4.5

Means and Standard Deviations of Variables in Analyses of Black Wives, by Age and Poverty Status: 1970

| | | Poverty Status | | | | | |
| | | All Wives | | Below 200% Pov. | | Above 200% Pov. | |
Age	Variable	Mean	S.D.	Mean	S.D.	Mean	S.D.
15–44	CEB	3,157	519	3,912	406	2,026	214
	Children under one year	131	21	167	27	84	19
	Age 20–29	383	33	371	35	408	45
	Low education	121	77	151	85	62	34
	Migration	181	99	171	101	198	98
	Never married*	371	47	400	45	298	41
	In school	34	13	30	14	40	18
	Labor force	571	74	447	91	738	75
20–29	CEB	2,190	320	2,817	265	1,371	175
	Children under one year	207	31	261	44	140	35
	Low education	68	50	94	60	25	17
	Migration	258	121	228	120	293	121
	Never married*	311	50	329	51	270	57
	In school	38	19	29	18	49	23
	Labor force	558	83	426	93	718	80
30–44	CEB	3,993	723	4,920	565	2,570	300
	Children under one year	59	17	77	21	34	15
	Low education	159	100	194	107	88	54
	Migration	121	84	119	86	128	89
	Never married*	93	27	101	30	78	31
	Labor force	599	75	474	102	764	79

*Never-married per 1,000 women in all marital statuses.

Note: See Table 4.1 for mean program enrollment per SAU and Table 4.6 for number of SAUs in each group, by poverty.

Source: FPP Impact Study.

within each age group below the poverty cutoff and very low among wives above the poverty cutoff. Program enrollment is negatively and significantly related to CEB in all analyses of black wives 20-29 and 30-44. The large negative program effects among wives above and below the poverty cutoff in both age groups suggest that controlling levels of fertility prior to 1969–70, the year in which we measure program effects on fertility, will be important.

The principal finding of the table relevant to the analysis of program effects is that, as was true for whites in Table 4.4, all coefficients of the measure of 1969 program enrollment are negative and significant for all age groups and

TABLE 4.6

Effects on CEB per 1,000 Black Wives, by Age and Poverty Status: 1970

| | Age and Poverty Status | | | | | | | | |
| | 15–44 | | | 20–29 | | | 30–44 | | |
Independent Variable	All Wives	<200% Poverty	>200% Poverty	All Wives	<200% Poverty	>200% Poverty	All Wives	<200% Poverty	>200% Poverty
Program enrollment	-.519*	-.740*	-.573*	-.524*	-.751*	-.525*	-.568*	-.772*	-.724*
Age 20–29	-1.113*	-1.851*	-.631*	n.i.	n.i.	n.i.	n.i.	n.i.	n.i.
Space	108.987*	55.645*	3.122	67.687*	-.032	-33.144*	179.820*	150.119*	-1.999
Low education	3.077*	1.758*	-.559	2.469*	1.152*	-.019	3.798*	2.137*	.545
Migration	-.228	-.051	.007	-.784*	-.454*	-.173	-1.156*	-1.060*	-.376
Never married	2.526*	2.522*	1.298*	.092	.765*	-.268	-1.156	-1.251	-1.199
In school	.899	-.202	-.622	-1.267*	-2.166*	-.599	n.i.	n.i.	n.i.
Labor force	-.712*	-.661*	-.332	-.254*	-.136	.104	-1.621*	-1.311*	-.433
R^2	.86	.63	.16	.76	.34	.09	.81	.54	.09
Number of SAUs	237	237	236	236	223	211	237	234	225

*$p < .05$.

Note: Ordinary least-squares regressions, unstandardized coefficients.

n.i. = not included in equation.

Source: FPP Impact Study.

66

for wives above and below the poverty cutoff. We view this as evidence of the outcome of a selection process related to attitudes toward, and provision of, birth control by physicians and hospitals in different communities in the post-World War II period. These factors affected upper-income and lower-income wives of both races. Communities with greater experience in the provision of birth control services were more likely than other communities to take advantage of the initiation of federal funding in the mid-1960s. Because they had an earlier start in program development, they had more patients in 1969. Because they had more patients in 1969, we have an apparent program effect on cumulative measures of fertility that is misleading because the number of patients in the 1969 program could not have sharply reduced, in any direct way, fertility prior to 1969.

Utilization of an annual fertility measure in testing for program effects should remove many of the ambiguities found with cumulative fertility measures. At the same time a genuine test of the effect of patients per 1,000 women in need requires not only an annual fertility measure, but one that can be specified to the population subgroup from which the program draws its patients—low-income and marginal-income women. If program effects are genuine, the analysis of annual fertility rates should reveal significant coefficients for the program variable on fertility among low-income and marginal-income women, but only small effects or none at all among higher-income women.* If the negative coefficient of the program variable on the fertility of women with high income is equal to the negative coefficient of women in the target population, the "program effect" probably would be spurious and due to the type of medical practice in the community rather than to the size of the patient caseload.

NOTE

1. For evidence of differences in contraceptive advice provided by physicians and health institutions, see A. Guttmacher, "Conception control and medical practice: the attitude of 3,381 physicians toward contraception and the contraceptives they prescribe," *Human Fertility*, 12

---

*This statement refers only to the direct effects of program activity, not to the indirect ones. Conceivably a family planning program could affect the fertility of higher-income women who are not clinic patients by disseminating information about contraception and legitimating the practice of fertility control. For discussion of these possible effects, see F. S. Jaffe, "Issues in the demographic evaluation of domestic family planning programs, in J. R. Udry and E. E. Huyck, eds., *The Demographic Evaluation of Domestic Family Planning Programs* (Cambridge, Mass.: Ballinger, 1975), p. 19.

(March): 1-11, 1947; S. Spivack, "Family planning in medical practice," in C. Kiser, ed., *Research in Family Planning* (Princeton, N.J.: Princeton University Press, 1962), pp. 193–210; and F. S. Jaffe, "Family planning service in the United States," in C. F. Westoff and R. Park, Jr., eds., *Aspects of Population Growth Policy,* vol. VI of U.S. Commission on Population Growth and the American Future, *Commission Research Reports* (Washington, D.C.: U.S. Government Printing Office, 1972), p. 205. On sterilization see N. Phillips, "The prevalence of surgical sterilization in a suburban population," *Demography,* 8:261–70, 1971; A. Leader, "The Houston Story: a vasectomy service in a family planning clinic," *Family Planning Perspectives,* 3:46–49, 1971; and P. K. Whelpton, A. A. Campbell, and J. E. Patterson, *Fertility and Family Planning in the United States* (Princeton, N.J.: Princeton University Press, 1966). On induced abortion see E. Weinstock, C. Tietze, F. S. Jaffe, and J. G. Dryfoos, "Legal abortion in the United States since the 1973 Supreme Court decision," *Family Planning Perspectives,* 7:23–31, 1975.

**PROGRAM EFFECTS ON
MARITAL FERTILITY**

In this chapter we estimate program effects on marital fertility, as measured by the number of children under one year per 1,000 wives living with a husband, derived from the 1970 census.* We examine the program's effects on marital fertility before testing effects on general fertility for two reasons: (1) marital fertility constitutes the greatest proportion of general fertility, and (2) separate analysis of marital fertility permits us to assess whether the resulting estimates of program effects are reasonable when compared with data for married women from the 1970 National Fertility Study (NFS).

The variable "1969 parity" is always included in equations estimating program effects on 1969 fertility. The inclusion of this control variable may result in conservative estimates of program effects because of the nature of a family planning program. A program is not a one-shot treatment (such as an immunization effort) but, rather, a continuous application of resources (personnel, funds, facilities) to produce services, information, and educational outputs; it is, therefore, subject to growth and development. Measurement of a family planning program's level of enrollment in a particular year differentiates between areas and thereby taps historical factors affecting program development. As a result, all of the measured effects of the program enrollment measure on CEB or on 1969 parity cannot be dismissed as spurious or unreal.

---

*Program enrollment effects on children under one year in 1970 refer to the effects of patients in organized family planning programs on the fertility of the population served by the 1969 program. In this chapter we use the term "1969 marital fertility" rather than 1969–70 to refer to children under one year at the time of the 1970 census. About 71 percent of these births occurred in 1969. The number of legitimate births in the January 1, 1969–April 1969 period was about equal to the number in the January 1, 1970–April 1970 period.

Introduction of "parity 1969" may, therefore, overcontrol the 1969 program effect on 1969–70 births and deflate it as a measure of current program impact. Since these two different but plausibly complementary effects cannot be sorted out, we have no choice but to use the analysis controlling the pre-1969 fertility level as our primary test of 1969 program impact.* Eliminating pre-1969 program effects deflates program enrollment coefficients and thus provides a rigorous test for program effects. If the analysis shows significant program effects using this control, we can feel safe in concluding that the program has had an impact, and perhaps that our coefficients understate it.

Regression coefficients for the program enrollment variable are therefore taken as a measure of program effects on the rate of children under one year when "parity 1969" is included in the equations. Because the program measure is not endogenous, its effect on children under one year can be estimated from recursive equations.

PROGRAM EFFECTS ON WHITE WIVES, BY AGE AND POVERTY

Table 5.1 shows the effects of independent variables on the number of children under one year among white wives aged 15-44, 20-29, and 30-44.† Among wives 15-44 in all poverty statuses (column 1), age structure, low education, migration, the proportion never married, and "parity 1969" have significant positive effects, and school enrollment a significant negative effect. The variable of interest is the unstandardized coefficient related to program enrollment. This coefficient is negative but not significant when all socioeconomic classes are combined, but it is negative and significant below the poverty cutoff (column 2), and positive but insignificant above the poverty cutoff (column 3). This pattern suggests that the program affects only women in the target population, a finding that would be expected if the program reduces fertility rates among patients. The right-hand panel shows a similar pattern of effects by SES on the fertility of white wives 30-44. In the center panel,

---

*Equations excluding the "parity 1969" control provide unstandardized regression coefficients of the program enrollment variable that include effects of pre-1969 community differences in health system attitudes toward and experience with birth control. These program enrollment coefficients generally are larger than those from equations that include 1969 parity controls, as should be expected.

†Analysis of teen-age marital fertility is treated in the section "Program Effects on Teen-Age Marital Fertility." Only 8 percent of black and 11 percent of white women 15-19 were married and living with a husband. This fact and other special aspects of married teen-agers require separate analyses.

TABLE 5.1

Effects on Children Under One Year per 1,000 White Wives, by Age and Poverty Status: 1970

Independent Variable	Age and Poverty Status								
	15-44			20-29			30-44		
	All Wives	<200% Poverty	>200% Poverty	All Wives	<200% Poverty	>200% Poverty	All Wives	<200% Poverty	>200% Poverty
Program enrollment	-.006**	-.014*	.002	-.033*	-.054*	-.019*	-.005	-.018*	.002
Age 20-29	.253*	.299*	.233*	n.i.	n.i.	n.i.	n.i.	n.i.	n.i.
Space	-1.526*	-5.402*	-2.489*	-.972	-4.910*	-2.676*	-2.054*	-3.405*	-2.019*
Low education	.026*	-.002	.040*	-.096*	-.089*	-.245*	.011*	.014*	.015
Migration	.021*	.048*	.015*	.046*	.065*	.044*	.030*	.023*	.031*
Never married	.098*	.024	.093*	.205*	.162*	.200*	.189*	.200*	.130*
In school	-.123*	-.093*	-.115*	-.102*	-.207*	-.012	n.i.	n.i.	n.i.
Labor force	-.009**	.018	-.016*	-.067*	-.084*	-.054*	.009*	.009	-.000
Parity 1969	.038*	.046*	.042*	.071*	.057*	.094*	.025*	.029*	.018*
R^2	.68	.47	.72	.48	.35	.53	.57	.42	.52

*$p < .05$.
**$p < .07$.

Notes: Number of SAUs is 778 in all analyses. See Table 4.3 for means and standard deviations. Ordinary least-squares regressions, unstandardized coefficients.

n.i. = not included in equations.

Source: FPP Impact Study.

however, we find significant and negative program effects among wives 20-29 both above and below the poverty cutoff; but the coefficient for lower-SES wives is nearly three times larger than for wives above the cutoff.

This pattern of program effects provides evidence that family planning programs reduce white fertility. White wives below the poverty cutoff who live in areas with more active programs have lower fertility than similar wives in areas with less active programs or no program at all. No systematic evidence of program effects on white wives above the poverty cutoff is shown.

PROGRAM EFFECTS ON BLACK WIVES, BY AGE AND POVERTY

Table 5.2 shows the results of comparable equations testing the effects of independent variables on the number of children under one year for black wives aged 15-44, by poverty level. Program enrollment takes a negative and significant relationship to fertility of wives in all SES levels, a much stronger and more significant negative coefficient among wives below the poverty cutoff, and a small and insignificant negative coefficient for black wives above the cutoff.

In the center panel we find a large negative and significant program coefficient for all wives aged 20-29 (column 4); but this effect is much stronger among wives below the poverty cutoff (column 5), and no significant effect above the poverty cutoff is shown (column 6). In the right-hand panel a large negative coefficient is related to the program variable only among black wives aged 30-44 who are below the poverty cutoff (column 8).

Whether the age groups are considered separately or together, the pattern of program effects on the fertility of black wives is quite similar to that among white wives.

PROGRAM EFFECTS ON WHITE WIVES, BY AGE AND INCOME

Because family size and family income jointly determine whether a family will be classified as below or above the poverty cutoff, possibly the high levels of fertility of wives below the poverty cutoff, compared with those above it (Table 4.3), are a function of the way poverty is defined. Furthermore, within the group classified as below 200 percent of poverty, program effects may be stronger on wives with more income than on those with less income. To test these issues, we now analyze program effects when wives are classified by family income alone, an analysis that should show whether or not any signifi-

TABLE 5.2

Effects on Children Under One Year per 1,000 Black Wives, by Age and Poverty Status: 1970

Age and Poverty Status

Independent Variable	15–44			20–29			30–44		
	All Wives (1)	Below 200% Pov. (2)	Above 200% Pov. (3)	All Wives (4)	Below 200% Pov. (5)	Above 200% Pov. (6)	All Wives (7)	Below 200% Pov. (8)	Above 200% Pov. (9)
Program enrollment	-.027*	-.046*	-.014	-.068*	-.097*	-.025	.001	-.029**	.006
Age 20–29	.216*	.291*	.125*	n.i.	n.i.	n.i.	n.i.	n.i.	n.i.
Space	-.251	-2.894*	-1.936*	1.064	-4.883*	-3.940	-.843	-2.215	.238
Low education	.036	-.037	.091*	.110**	-.009	.089	.026	.019	.010
Migration	-.014	.002	.013	-.007	.060	.013	.013	.010	.013
Never married	-.036	-.052	.029	.092*	.179*	-.026	-.020	-.059	.049
In school	.186*	.171	.259*	.036	.090	-.032*	n.i.	n.i.	n.i.
Labor force	-.021	-.013	-.045*	-.042	-.017	-.096*	-.020	-.031	-.035*
Parity 1969	.025*	.030*	.015*	.013	.027*	.003	-.012*	.011*	.009*
R^2	.47	.22	.19	.24	.10	.10	.35	.12	.07
Number of SAUs	237	237	236	236	223	210	237	234	224

*p < .05. **p < .09.

Notes: See Table 4.5 for means and standard deviations. Ordinary least-squares regressions, unstandardized coefficients.

n.i. = not included in equation

Source: FPP Impact Study.

cant bias in estimating program effects is introduced when wives are classified by poverty status.

We divide white and black wives into three groups: (1) those whose family income was less than 50 percent of U.S. median family income in 1969; (2) those whose family income was between 50 and 99 percent of median family income; and (3) those whose family income was higher than median family income. Wives in families with higher-than-median income are not always the same as those in families above 200 percent of poverty.

A comparison of the fertility statistics in tables 4.3 and 5.3 reveals differences in fertility and other characteristics related to the way SES is defined. For example, wives aged 30-44 below and above 200 percent of poverty had 4,018 and 2,683 children ever born, respectively (Table 4.3). The differences in children ever born to wives 30-44 are much smaller when wives are classified by family income alone (Table 5.3). This is also true in the other age groups. Differences in children under one year per 1,000 wives also are smaller when wives are classified by income alone than by poverty status. Classification by family income, therefore, results in SES groups that have more homogeneous levels of fertility than classification by poverty status.

Since we have no direct information on the income of 1969 family planning patients, but only on their poverty status, we will assume here that they were generally drawn from families with income below the 1969 median ($9,433) and that few patients had more than median income. We now test the view that the previously estimated program effects in the group below the poverty cutoff emerge because of the way the women were classified.

In Table 5.4 the regression coefficients measuring program impact on white wives aged 15-44 indicate negative and significant effects among wives in both subgroups below median income; no significant effects on wives above median income are shown. The same finding emerges for white wives aged 20-29, while for wives 30-44 negative and statistically significant effects are found only in the income class between 50 and 99 percent of median. The sign and significance of the program coefficients fit the expected pattern, indicating program effects in all age groups; the two lower-income groups show negative signs that are significant in five of six comparisons. None of the three upper-income group coefficients differ significantly from zero.

PROGRAM EFFECTS ON BLACK WIVES, BY AGE AND INCOME

Means and standard deviations used in a comparable analysis of black wives, classified by age and family income alone, are shown in Table 5.5. Comparing means of fertility variables in this table with those for black wives below and above 200 percent of poverty (Table 4.5) shows again that fertility

TABLE 5.3

Means and Standard Deviations of Variables in Analyses of White Wives, by Age and Income Group: 1970

	Income Group					
	Under 50% Med. Inc.		50–99% Med. Inc.		100%+ Med. Inc.	
Variable	Mean	S. D.	Mean	S. D.	Mean	S. D.
15–44						
CEB	2,118	424	2,298	289	2,467	297
Child < one year	180	32	147	24	82	14
Age 20–29	465	68	493	52	315	34
Low education	99	84	51	43	21	18
Migration	365	129	313	107	273	82
Never married	314	72	219	41	295	44
In school	59	48	25	17	25	10
Labor force	276	64	337	78	511	74
20–29						
CEB	1,559	330	1,667	201	1,475	187
Child < one year	241	47	218	32	172	28
Low education	68	67	28	26	12	11
Migration	459	145	401	116	411	100
Never married	247	105	117	54	219	71
In school	69	68	31	24	34	17
Labor force	289	80	340	86	508	81
30–44						
CEB	3,373	431	3,151	345	2,963	344
Child < one year	60	26	57	16	38	10
Low education	161	121	76	61	26	22
Migration	224	98	214	96	208	75
Never married	96	36	54	33	32	20
Labor force	250	57	328	77	513	76

Note: See Table 5.4 for number of SAUs in each subgroup.
Source: FPP Impact Study.

is relatively more homogeneous when income alone, rather than poverty, is used as the classification criterion. However, black wives with more than median income in all age groups have substantially higher CEB, and somewhat higher rates of children under one year, than wives above 200 percent of poverty. These fertility differences by family income do not differentiate fertility by the level of husband's income alone; labor force participation of black wives increases rapidly across income groups.

TABLE 5.4

Effects on Children Under One Year per 1,000 White Wives, by Age and Income Group: 1970

Independent Variable	Income Group		
	Under 50% Median	50–99% of Median	· 100% + Median
15–44			
Program enrollment	−.047*	−.030*	.002
Age 20–29	−.281*	.402*	.225*
Space	−2.237*	−5.571*	−2.697*
Low education	−.013	−.042*	.032
Migration	.031*	−.011	.033*
Never married	.011	.068*	.078*
In school	−.282*	−.176*	−.064*
Labor force	.003	−.022*	−.028*
Parity 1969	.018*	.060*	.030*
R^2	.20	.60	.67
Number of SAUs	778	778	778
20–29			
Program enrollment	−.076*	−.066*	−.012
Space	1.323	−6.644*	−4.858*
Low education	−.001	−.210*	−.202*
Migration	.035*	.024*	−.065*
Never married	.083*	.163*	.159*
In school	−.274*	.109*	−.105*
Labor force	−.074*	−.072*	−.078*
Parity 1969	.003	.093*	.069*
R^2	.17	.38	.40
Number of SAUs	738	778	778
30–44			
Program enrollment	−.005	−.019*	.001
Space	−1.356	−3.462*	−1.857*
Low education	−.000	−.023*	.011
Migration	.036*	.016*	.030*
Never married	.154*	.146*	.152*
Labor force	−.065*	.005	−.013*
Parity 1969	.025*	.028*	.017*
R^2	.19	.38	.47
Number of SAUs	696	778	778

*$p < .05$.
Note: Ordinary least-squares regressions, unstandardized coefficients.
Source: FPP Impact Study.

Table 5.6 displays regression coefficients for black wives, by age and family income. The patterns are identical with those reported for whites in Table 5.4. Among wives aged 15-44 and 20-29, the program enrollment measure is negative and statistically significant in the two lower-income groups, but not significant in the above-median income group. Among black wives aged 30-44, it is negative and significant among wives with 50-99 percent of

TABLE 5.5

Means and Standard Deviations of Variables in Analyses of Black Wives, by Age and Income Group: 1970

	Income Group					
	Under 50% Med. Inc.		50-99% Med. Inc.		100%+ Med. Inc.	
Variable	Mean	S. D.	Mean	S. D.	Mean	S. D.
15–44						
CEB	3,247	689	3,203	478	2,873	359
Child < one year	180	39	134	27	88	24
Age 20-29	411	56	406	46	337	48
Low education	190	100	106	56	63	42
Migration	188	112	180	108	178	91
Never married	402	47	337	49	371	49
In school	39	23	28	14	41	19
Labor force	371	74	549	119	767	64
20–29						
CEB	2,499	414	2,229	271	1,737	225
Child < one year	254	44	207	43	151	33
Low education	130	79	51	30	28	25
Migration	226	111	247	124	283	116
Never married	343	50	255	56	342	69
In school	31	24	32	21	54	28
Labor force	369	80	555	115	757	64
30–44						
CEB	4,456	909	4,069	649	3,517	505
Child < one year	74	30	61	21	45	21
Low education	291	120	150	79	81	57
Migration	103	72	121	95	123	86
Never married	134	37	69	27	73	32
Labor force	394	84	557	134	784	71

Note: See Table 5.6 for number of SAUs in each subgroup.
Source: FPP Impact Study.

TABLE 5.6

Effects on Children Under One Year per 1,000 Black Wives, by Age and Income Group: 1970

Independent Variable	Income Group		
	Under 50% Median	50–99% Median	100% + Median
15–44			
Program enrollment	−.071*	−.057*	−.015
Age 20–29	.175*	.244*	.138*
Space	1.210	−1.638	1.482
Low education	.048	−.069	.137*
Migration	.056	.031	−.004
Never married	.041	−.045	.072
In school	.379*	−.044	.185*
Labor force	−.043	−.067*	−.052*
Parity 1969	.007	.015*	−.005
R^2	.19	.29	.17
Number of SAUs	222	237	228
20–29			
Program enrollment	−.078*	−.082*	−.030
Space	1.662	−4.777*	−.326
Low education	.087	−.010	.116
Migration	.021	−.011	.011
Never married	.143*	.029	−.064
In school	.040	−.027	.039
Labor force	.007	−.120*	−.074
Parity 1969	.009	.021	.000
R^2	.13	.15	.06
Number of SAUs	168	226	155
30–44			
Program enrollment	−.023	−.043*	.011
Space	−3.415	−1.324	2.131
Low education	.045*	−.002	.025
Migration	−.041	−.012	.000
Never married	−.056	.015	.044
Labor force	−.005	−.026*	−.068*
Parity 1969	.013*	.004	.005
R^2	.26	.06	.08
Number of SAUs	171	232	211

*$p < .05$.

Note: Ordinary least-squares regressions, unstandardized coefficients.
Source: FPP Impact Study.

median income, but not significant in the lowest-income group* or above median income.

Among black wives we also conclude that higher levels of program enrollment are related to lower levels of fertility in the population from which patients are drawn, net of a number of other characteristics related to fertility.

PROGRAM EFFECTS ON WHITE WIVES IN WHITE SAUs

Since the program activity measure includes both white and black patients, the program effects reported above on white fertility can be questioned. Direct control on this problem is possible by excluding from the analysis SAUs in which white wives represent less than 90 percent of all wives in each age and poverty status group. In the remaining "white SAUs" the average proportion of white wives is 96 to 97 percent, and almost all patients and women in need must be white. As a result the possible confounding effects of nonwhite patients in measuring program impact on white fertility in all SAUs is reduced. Analysis of white SAUs, therefore, should provide a better measure of the program's impact on white fertility.

Equations testing program effects on fertility of white wives, by age and poverty status, who live in white SAUs yielded results similar to those reported in Table 5.1 and are not presented in detail so as to conserve space; rather, we summarize them in Table 5.7 below. The major difference is that the program enrollment coefficients in the white-SAU analysis were larger than in the all-SAU analysis. The white-SAU analysis thus confirmed and strengthened the finding of significant program effects on the fertility of lower-SES white wives.

PRELIMINARY SUMMARY

Table 5.7 brings together the unstandardized regression coefficients of the program enrollment variable for different subgroups of wives by age, race, income, and poverty classification. It shows a consistent pattern of program effects regardless of which SES classification scheme is utilized. We conclude that classification of wives by their relationship to the federal poverty index does not introduce any bias that would contribute to finding spurious program effects.

---

*This finding also applied to white wives aged 30-44 below 50 percent of median income, and may be due to low participation by this age-income class in the program because of a differential access to the program that is related to characteristics of wives in this subgroup.

TABLE 5.7

Summary of Program Enrollment Effects on Children Under One Year, per 1,000 Wives, by Age, Race, and SES: 1970

Socioeconomic Classification	Race								
	White Wives (all SAUs)				Black Wives		
	15–44	20–29	30–44		15–44	20–29	30–44
Under 200% poverty	−.014*	−.054*	−.018*		−.046*	−.097*	−.029**
Above 200% poverty	.002	−.019*	.002		−.014	−.025	.006
Under 50% median income	−.047*	−.076*	−.005		−.071*	−.078*	−.023
50–99% median income	−.030*	−.066*	−.018*		−.057*	−.082*	−.043*
Above 100% median income	.002	−.012	.001		−.016	−.030	−.011
	White Wives (white SAUs only)						
Below 200% poverty	−.031*	−.077*	−.027*				
Above 200% poverty	−.006	−.006	−.005				

*p < .05.
**p < .09.
Note: Ordinary least-squares regressions, unstandardized coefficients.
Source: FPP Impact Study.

80

The program had negative effects on marital fertility in all lower-income or poverty subgroups, and these effects were statistically significant in 18 of 21 comparisons. The program enrollment coefficients were not significant in 14 of 15 subgroups of upper-SES wives.

The coefficients among lower-income wives are always larger in the 20-29 age group than in the other two. They are smaller for wives 30-44 in six of seven comparisons with wives aged 15-44. These are both sensible patterns by age, given age differences in fertility rates and the absolute size of the rates represented by birth planning failures (see Tables 5.12 and 5.13 below).

Black coefficients are higher than white coefficients in all lower-income comparisons between comparable age groups. This too is reasonable, because a higher proportion of black births than white births are planning failures.

PROGRAM EFFECTS ON TEEN-AGE MARITAL FERTILITY

Analysis of program effects on teen-age marital fertility is more difficult than similar studies of older age groups. Only a small proportion of teen-agers are married. Within a given SAU the number of married teen-agers often is too small to allow reliable analysis of white and black poverty-specific data. SAUs have considerable attrition, and only a small number of unrepresentative SAUs are available for some analyses. Small sample size leads to unstable regression coefficients. A second problem is related to use of "parity 1969" in teen-age studies. In this chapter we examine teen-age marital fertility, while in chapter 6 we deal with overall teen-age fertility.

Table 5.8 provides means and standard deviations for white and black teen-age wives in SAUs with more than 300 wives in a given subgroup. In both racial groups wives below 200 percent of poverty have, as expected, more children ever born and children under one year than wives above the poverty cutoff. Both measures of fertility, however, are higher among blacks in each SES than among comparable whites.

White and black teen-age wives below the poverty cutoff have lower educational attainment than those above. School enrollment is somewhat higher among whites below than above the cutoff, while the reverse is true among blacks. In all comparisons labor force participation is higher among wives above than below the poverty cutoff. Migration is higher for whites below than above the cutoff, a pattern reversed among blacks.

The mean number of patients per 1,000 women in need (program enrollment) varies across groups as a function of selection. In the 744 SAUs with sufficient cases to analyze whites in all poverty groups, the mean is only slightly higher than the national SAU mean. But SAUs containing enough teen-age white wives below or above the poverty cutoff for analysis have higher program enrollment rates than average. This effect is a function of the more developed programs being located in areas with larger populations. Among blacks the 96

TABLE 5.8

Means and Standard Deviations of Variables in Analyses of Wives Aged 15–19, by Race and Poverty Status: 1970

Variable	Statistic	White Wives			Black Wives		
		All Poverty	Below 200%	Above 200%	All Poverty	Below 200%	Above 200%
Program enrollment	Mean	84	106	108	177	197	345
	S.D.	111	123	126	139	143	153
CEB	Mean	597	687	483	1,076	1,198	750
	S.D.	94	125	90	142	137	99
Children under one year	Mean	287	345	208	367	402	259
	S.D.	55	67	58	67	78	45
Childless	Mean	519	464	595	296	249	418
	S.D.	66	78	71	58	57	61
Low education	Mean	42	67	29	109	140	46
	S.D.	41	58	25	77	83	22
Migration	Mean	362	398	334	206	182	247
	S.D.	114	136	108	106	78	103
Never married	Mean	853	777	876	877	881	874
	S.D.	54	68	49	22	20	36
In school	Mean	122	133	113	172	169	185
	S.D.	42	52	39	55	61	48
Labor force	Mean	353	276	435	342	281	447
	S.D.	84	81	94	90	82	66
Number of SAUs		744	450	446	96	66	16

Source: FPP Impact Study.

82

SAUs available for analysis of all poverty-status teen-age wives had a mean program enrollment rate of 177 per 1,000; in the 66 SAUs with enough cases below the poverty cutoff, the rate was 197, and the 16 SAUs with more than 300 black teen-age wives above the poverty cutoff had a mean of 345. Although these means of program enrollment differ from the national average, this should not necessarily bias estimates of program effects except when, as in the case of black wives classified by poverty, the small number of SAUs depresses the reliability and generality of the results.

In the following analyses we follow procedures similar to those used above for estimating program effects among older married women. In the case of teen-agers, however, the treatment of the 1969 parity measure as a control for the level of fertility prior to 1969 is more difficult. One-third to one-half of all children ever born to teen-age wives were born in the year for which the estimate of program effects is being attempted. Among wives still in the teen-age years, most of the children born before 1969 (the children in the 1969 parity measure) were born in 1967–68. This is close enough in time to our measure of program enrollment to raise doubts about including the parity measure as a control in equations estimating program effects on teen-age wives. In the analysis below we show the results with and without the parity control.

Analyses of White Teen-Age Wives

Table 5.9 displays unstandardized regression coefficients from equations for white teen-age wives. Taking 1969 parity as the first dependent variable (columns 1, 4, and 7), explained variance is .25 in analyses of all poverty groups, .36 below the poverty cutoff, and only .09 above it. Low education and marital status have positive and significant coefficients to 1969 parity in all three equations; migration and school enrollment have negative and significant coefficients in all groups. Space is positive in all equations, and significant in two of three. Labor force participation is negative in all groups, and significant in two of three equations. The program variable is not significant in any group, indicating little or no program effects on levels of fertility prior to 1969 among married white women still under 20 years in 1970.

Virtually no difference occurs in the program coefficient, which is negative in all six equations taking children under one year as the dependent variable, when 1969 parity is included or omitted from the equations. The program coefficient is significant in analysis for teen-age wives in all poverty statuses (columns 2 and 3) and for those above the poverty cutoff (columns 8 and 9).

Our general conclusion is that areas with more clinic patients had lower 1969 white teen-age marital fertility than areas with fewer patients, net of other measured variables that affect teen-age marital fertility. The logic underlying these effects is not as simple as was the case for older wives. Teen-age wives above 200 percent of poverty have significant negative coefficients that are

TABLE 5.9

Effects on 1969 Parity and Children Under One Year per 1,000 White Wives Aged 15–19, by Poverty Status: 1970

Whites in All SAUs

Independent Variable	All Poverty			Below 200% of Poverty			Above 200% of Poverty		
	Parity 1969 (1)	Child < 1 yr. (2)	Child < 1 yr. (3)	Parity 1969 (4)	Child < 1 yr. (5)	Child < 1 yr. (6)	Parity 1969 (7)	Child < 1 yr. (8)	Child < 1 yr. (9)
Program enrollment	.036	-.048*	-.046*	.018	-.014	-.013	.012	-.066*	-.066*
Space	11.815*	1.172	2.088	1.380	-8.137*	-8.131*	10.175*	-3.697	-3.467
Low education	.374*	-.101*	-.073	.353*	-.121*	-.120*	.477*	-.184*	-.173*
Migration	-.208*	-.078*	-.094*	-.222*	-.043*	-.044*	-.095*	-.091*	-.093*
Never married	.167*	.354*	.366*	.278*	.372*	.373*	.190*	.436*	.441*
In school	-.202*	-.307*	-.324*	-.222*	-.354*	-.355*	-.224*	-.270*	-.276*
Labor force	-.092*	-.122*	-.129*	-.099*	-.019	-.019	-.040	-.182*	-.183*
Parity 1969	n.i.	n.i.	-.078*	n.i.	n.i.	-.038	n.i.	n.i.	-.023
R^2	.25	.31	.32	.36	.34	.34	.09	.37	.37
Number of SAUs	744			450			446		

* $p < .05$.

Note: Ordinary least-squares regressions, unstandardized coefficients.

n.i. = not included in equation.

Source: FPP Impact Study

84

larger than those for wives below the poverty cutoff. For larger program effects in the group above the poverty cutoff, three plausible explanations apply only to the teen-age population. First, because the majority of these women are childless, and most wives with children have only one child, the income needed by the childless or one-child family to be above 200 percent of the poverty cutoff in 1969 was no more than $5,000 to $6,000.[1] In absolute terms this constitutes a limited income, and evidence indicates that some young wives in this income range use organized family planning facilities. Second, wives of college students (or college students who are wives) constitute a substantial part of the teen-age married population above the poverty cutoff, and this group also participates in clinic programs. Third, teen-age patients above the poverty cutoff may be more effective contraceptors than those below the cutoff. For these reasons the program coefficients may actually measure a reasonable pattern of program effects among married teen-agers, and the preferred measure of program impact on teen-age wives may be the coefficient derived from analysis of wives in all poverty statuses.

White Teen-Age Marital Fertility, By Family Income

If, as we suggest, 200 percent of poverty does not provide an adequate cutting point to divide teen-agers who may be patients in organized programs from those who are not, the measure of program enrollment should take negative coefficients for wives with family incomes below the 1969 median income in the United States, but be insignificant above that level. Because young wives tend to have limited incomes, married female patients are most likely to have been drawn from wives below median income, and few teen-age wives were likely to have incomes above the median.

The number of SAUs available for analysis of white teen-age wives declines drastically when the median income level is exceeded (Table 5.10). Thus, while 446 SAUs had more than 300 white wives over 200 percent of poverty, only 90 SAUs had 300 or more teen-age white wives above median income. The lower panel of Table 5.10 shows the means and standard deviations of variables used in the analysis of program effects on teen-age marital fertility, by family income. The pattern of the three fertility measures across the three income groups seems reasonable. The higher the CEB, the lower the number per 1,000 wives who are childless. The rate of children under one year is somewhat higher among the two subgroups below than among wives above median income, as one might expect. Labor force participation and low education also show their expected pattern in relation to family income status. The program enrollment variable is higher than the national average because of the selection of SAUs with larger populations required in analysis of this subgroup of wives. Migration rates decline as family income increases, while the rate of

TABLE 5.10

Effects on Children Under One Year per 1,000 White Wives Aged 15—19, by Income Group: 1970

	Income Group					
	Under 50% Med.		50—99% Median		100%+ Median	
Independent Variable	Omit Parity	Include Parity	Omit Parity	Include Parity	Omit Parity	Include Parity
	Unstandardized Coefficients					
Program enrollment	-.036	-.036	-.113*	-.115*	.002	.008
Space	-4.237*	-4.358*	-11.554*	-12.079*	-.282	.687
Low education	.042	.012	-.198*	-.215*	-.009	.079
Migration	-.015	-.007	-.060*	-.053*	.048	.052
Never married	.186*	.180*	.203*	.198*	.863*	.933*
In school	-.190*	-.182*	-.247*	-.238*	-.193	-.227*
Labor force	-.015	-.010	-.142*	-.139*	-.204*	-.220*
Parity 1969	n.i.	.054	n.i.	.047	n.i.	-.098*
R^2	.18	.19	.25	.26	.18	.20
No. of SAUs	315		424		90	

	Means and Standard Deviations					
	Mean	St.D.	Mean	St.D.	Mean	St.D.
Program enrollment	127	133	110	126	204	162
CEB	543	116	620	107	527	92
Childless	554	74	496	73	593	58
Children < one year	293	60	282	64	223	51
Low education	67	62	42	37	37	27
Migration	425	147	345	112	281	102
Never married	656	100	766	63	948	21
In school	141	58	99	40	139	46
Labor force	286	84	374	99	463	76

$^*p < .05$.

Note: Ordinary least-squares regressions, unstandardized coefficients.

n.i. = not included in equation.

Source: FPP Impact Study

teen-age women never married, when classified by family income, increases across family income intervals; very few women aged 15-19 in families above the median family income are married.

The upper panel reports the regression analysis, by family income level, first excluding and then including 1969 parity. Including the parity measure has little effect on any teen-age subgroup. The program coefficient is negative but not significant in the group below 50 percent of median income, and negative and significant in the group with 50-99 percent of median income. Above median income the program coefficient is about zero. This pattern of program effects by family income is quite similar to the pattern of program effects among older white age groups. It suggests, perhaps, more effective use (or perhaps just more use) of clinic services by teen-age wives in the 50-99 percent of median income interval than by those below that range. We conclude that this analysis supports the view that family planning programs reduced the fertility of white teen-age wives in 1969.

Analyses of Black Teen-Age Wives

Table 5.11 shows regression coefficients in analyses of 1969 parity and children under one year for black teen-age wives. Because so few SAUs are available, neither of the two large coefficients of program enrollment in the analysis of 1969 parity are significant, although the negative direction of these effects on 1969 parity is expected. Low education is related to higher 1969 parity, while migration and school enrollment and later age at marriage (high proportions single) are related to lower 1969 parity. Marital status turns positive in analysis of children under one year, as was also found among whites. Labor force participation and space have no appreciable relationship to 1969 parity.

In both equations for children under one year in the all-poverty status group, the variable with the largest standardized coefficient, and the one nearest to statistical significance, is the program measure. It is negative in equations both including and excluding 1969 parity.*

In the 66 SAUs with enough black wives below poverty for study, the program coefficient remains negative. The standard error of these coefficients is considerably greater than when all poverty SAUs were used, and the all-poverty coefficient should, therefore, provide a better estimate of program effects. No analyses were attempted of the 16 SAUs with 300 or more black

---

*Because such a high proportion of teen-age brides are pregnant at the time of marriage, a large portion of the children ever born to wives in this age group were conceived out of wedlock. Both children in the 1969 parity measure and children under one year could have been conceived out of wedlock. Thus, a note of interest is that the program variable is positively related (data not shown) to childlessness among both black and white teen-age wives. This suggests that the negative effect of the program variable on children under one year was possibly a function of premarital birth control services provided by family planning clinics.

TABLE 5.11

Effects on 1969 Parity and Children Under One Year per 1,000 Black Wives Aged 15–19, by Poverty Status: 1970

Independent Variable	All Poverty			Below Poverty		
	Parity 1969	Children Under 1 yr.	Children Under 1 yr.	Parity 1969	Children Under 1 yr.	Children Under 1 yr.
Program enrollment	-.192	-.113[a]	-.133[b]	-.140	-.081[c]	-.099[d]
Space	-2.143	-.929	-1.145	-32.029	-7.061	-11.128
Low education	.373	.113	.150	.350	-.020	.065
Migration	-.229	-.006	.029	-.149	.110	.091
Never married	-.329	.400	.367	.660	.443	.527
In school	-.123	.036	.023	-.103	.123	.110
Labor force	.051	-.017	-.012	.340	-.091	-.048
Parity 1969	n.i.	n.i.	-.101	n.i.	n.i.	-.127
R^2	.15	.07	.11	.10	.07	.11
Number of SAUs	96			66		

[a] $p = .18$ and standardized coefficient is -.196, the largest in this set.
[b] $p = .12$ and standardized coefficient is -.229, the largest in this set.
[c] $p = .56$ and standardized coefficient is -.123, the second largest in this set.
[d] $p = .48$ and standardized coefficient is -.150, the third largest in this set.

Notes: The analysis omits the 16 SAUs with 300 or more wives above poverty. Ordinary least-squares regressions, unstandardized coefficients.

n.i = not included in equation

Source: FPP Impact Study.

teen-age wives above the poverty cutoff. Because so few black teen–age wives have incomes above 200 percent of poverty and a substantial number of these black teen-age wives may be patients, using the all-poverty program coefficient, rather than poverty-specific coefficients, is additionally justified for estimating program effects among black teen-age wives.

TESTING THE PLAUSIBILITY OF ESTIMATES OF PROGRAM EFFECTS ON MARITAL FERTILITY

Family planning programs can only prevent births that are not wanted or are mistimed. For each age, race, and SES we can estimate the proportion of children under one year per 1,000 wives that were wanted and the proportion of such births that the wives would have preferred to have delayed or prevented during the period under study. For these estimates we use data from the 1970 NFS that report the proportion of 1968–70 births defined by married women in that study to be timing or number failures.* A timing failure is a birth that usually would have been preferred at a later time. A number failure is a birth not wanted at any time. Since the categories are mutually exclusive, the sum of births defined as timing or number failures, when divided by the total number of births, is the proportion of total births that were planning failures. Because patients in family planning programs are women who either desire to delay a birth or do not want one at any time in the future, it is appropriate to use the total planning failure rate for the 1968–70 period to check out estimates of the maximum likely effect on the number of children under one year a program serving all women in need could have had. Such an effect is, of course, hypothetical; the value of the extrapolation is that it permits a check of our estimates of program effects to be evaluated against an independent estimate of the expected reduction in fertility from improved control over fertility, and thus enables us to establish whether or not our estimates are plausible.

In Table 5.12 data for white wives are presented. Columns 1 and 2 report the number of SAUs and of children under one year in each subgroup analysis, while column 3 shows the estimated proportion of birth planning failures for

---

*Special tabulations of the 1970 NFS were supplied by C. F. Westoff and L. Paul of the Office of Population Research, Princeton University, and are reported in detail in Appendix B.

each subgroup.* Column 4 shows the expected reduction in the number of children under one year per 1,000 wives in each subgroup had no birth planning failures occurred. The procedure is straightforward; in the first row, for example, we multiply 172 by .400 and get 69, the estimated potential decline in the rate of children under one year if this group of wives could have regulated their fertility perfectly.

We are now in a position to judge whether our estimates of program effects are plausible. To estimate the maximum potential impact of the family planning program on fertility, we use the unstandardized program enrollment regression coefficients reported above. By moving the decimal point three places to the right, we have an estimate of the effect of the 1969 program on fertility, net of other factors, had all women in need been served. These data are shown in column 5. If the figure in column 5 were greater than that in column 4, we would indicate that the estimate of program effects might be too high (unless an argument is made that sampling error in the estimate of planning failures in column 3 could account for the discrepancy). Comparisons of columns 4 and 5 find no instance in which the extrapolated estimate of potential program effects on white wives is greater than the expected effects in the absence of birth planning failures, as reported to the 1970 NFS. We conclude that these estimates, while extrapolated beyond the range of observed program enrollment rates, appear reasonable.

Table 5.13 is a complementary analysis of the plausibility of estimated program effects on fertility of different types of black wives. Although we show data for black wives aged 15-19, classified by their relationship to median family income, we have no estimates of program effects for them because there are too few SAUs available for analysis (column 1).

Are the estimates of program effects on black fertility reasonable? Comparing column 5 with column 4, we again find no instance in which the extrapolated estimate of program effects exceeds the maximum expected effects if no wife had a birth planning failure. We conclude that our coefficients estimating the effect of the 1969 family planning program on black marital fertility, net of other factors, are also plausible.

---

*For wives below 200 percent of poverty, Appendix Table B.3 provides an adjusted estimate of the birth planning failure rate using 1970 NFS data. This adjustment was necessary because NFS data were specific to women below 150 percent of poverty, while our poverty cutoff was 200 percent. Because women between 150 and 200 percent of poverty are likely to have somewhat lower birth planning failure rates than women below 150 percent of poverty, some adjustment was required. The failure rates for wives under half of median income are identical to the rates shown in Appendix Table B.1 for women under $5,000 in the 1970 NFS. Since 1969 U.S. median family income was $9,433, our cutoff for below 50 percent of median is $4,716. This seems close enough to the $5,000 level used by NFS in Table B.1 for us to use the NFS estimate without adjustment to estimate the failure rate for women in our study who were under half of median income. We apply the failure rates from the 1970 NFS for women in the $5,000-$9,999 family income interval to wives in our study in the 50-99 percent of median income range.

TABLE 5.12

Expected Reductions in White Marital Fertility, Assuming Zero
Birth Planning Failures and All Women in Need Served by
Family Planning Programs: 1970

Age	Number of SAUs (1)	Children Under 1 year (2)	1968-70 Total Failures (3)	Expected Rate Reduction	
				Zero Planning Failures (4)	All in Need Served (5)
White Wives Below 200% of Poverty in All SAUs					
15—44	778	172	.400	−69	−14
15—19*	744	287	.419	−120	−46
20—29	778	272	.368	−100	−54
30—44	778	74	.532	−39	−18
White Wives Below 50% of Median Income					
15—44	778	180	.450	−81	−47
15—19	315	293	.421	−123	−36
20—29	738	241	.451	−109	−76
30—44	696	60	.474	−28	−5
White Wives Between 50 and 99% of Median Income					
15—44	778	147	.390	−57	−30
15—19	424	282	.411	−116	−115
20—29	778	218	.354	−77	−66
30—44	778	57	.540	−31	−18

*Uses all-poverty coefficient.
Sources: FPP Impact Study and 1970 NFS.

CONCLUSION

In this chapter we have documented a consistent pattern: increasing the
level of program enrollment reduces the fertility of low-SES white and black
wives in all age groups, net of other factors known to influence fertility. The
negative effect of program enrollment occurred among low-SES wives, but was
generally nonexistent in the population of women not served by the family
planning program. We conclude, therefore, that the evidence demonstrates
that the program reduces marital fertility among the patients it serves: the
greater the number of patients served, the greater will be the reduction of their
unwanted fertility.

TABLE 5.13

Expected Reductions in Black Marital Fertility, Assuming Zero
Birth Planning Failures and All Women in Need Served by
Family Planning Programs: 1970

				Expected Rate Reduction	
Age	Number of SAUs (1)	Children Under 1 year (2)	1968-70 Total Failures (3)	Zero Planning Failures (4)	All in Need Served (5)
	Black Wives Below 200% of Poverty in All SAUs				
15—44	237	167	.605	−101	−46
15—19	96[a]	367	.586	−215	−133
20—29	222	261	.585	−153	−97
30—44	234	77	.665	−51	−29
	Black Wives Below 50% of Median Income				
15—44	222	180	.579	−104	−71
15—19	31	395	.586	−231	b
20—29	168	254	.600	−152	−78
30—44	171	74	.533	−39	−23
	Black Wives Between 50 and 99% of Median Income				
15—44	237	134	.609	−82	−57
15—19	18	356	.560	−199	b
20—29	226	207	.583	−121	−82
30—44	232	61	.735	−45	−43

[a]Uses all-poverty coefficient.
[b]Not calculated because of small number of SAUs.
Sources: FPP Impact Study and 1970 NFS.

The study has shown program effects of varying magnitudes in the different low-SES subgroups of married women of childbearing age from which patients of organized family planning programs are primarily drawn. Comparison of the magnitude of these program effects with the proportions of all births to these subgroups in the period under study that were planning failures shows that our estimated effects are plausible, falling within the range of the fertility reduction that would have been expected if no planning failures had occurred.

NOTE

1. U.S. Bureau of the Census, *Statistical Abstract of the United States, 1976* (Washington, D.C.: U.S. Government Printing Office, 1976), Table 651.

6

PROGRAM EFFECTS
ON FERTILITY OF WOMEN
IN ALL MARITAL STATUSES

Our analysis of program effects thus far has been restricted to married women living with their husbands. The census also reported the number of children under one year for women in all marital statuses. As a result we can analyze program effects on the number of children under one year per 1,000 women in all marital statuses. Separate analyses of program effects on the fertility of never-married, separated, widowed, or divorced women are not possible.

Table 6.1 shows the extent to which the analysis of married wives living with their husbands omits women in other marital statuses. Among whites 648 out of every 1,000 women aged 15–44 were married and living with a spouse, compared with only 434 among blacks; the analysis of marital fertility thus omits about one-third of white women of reproductive age and more than half of blacks. Among teen-agers of both races, restricting analysis to marital fertility excludes about 90 percent of young women. Sharp racial differences occur in the 20–29 and 30–44 age groups partly because (1) a greater proportion of blacks than whites report themselves as never married, and (2) a smaller proportion of ever-married blacks than whites of comparable age are living with their husbands. The analysis of marital fertility includes nearly all white women aged 30–44 who actually bear children, but in the other age and racial groups many women are excluded.

Table 6.2 compares the count of children under one year in the average SAU who are living with married, spouse-present women with the number reported by women in all marital statuses. The count is always larger when the all-marital-status reports are used. Among whites the differences are relatively small, except for a 13 percent increase in the 15–19 age group. Among blacks all age groups have large differences. For blacks aged 15–44 the number of children under one year reported by women in all marital statuses is 52 percent greater than the number reported by married women living with a

TABLE 6.1

Mean SAU Rates for Married, Spouse-Present Women per 1,000 Women, by Race and Age: 1970

Race	15–44	15–19	20–29	30–44
White	648	115	730	855
Black	434	82	492	613

Source: FPP Impact Study.

husband, while among teen-agers more than twice as many black children are counted in the all-marital-status reports.

Thus, analysis of marital fertility omits a substantial part of total fertility, especially among blacks, because a significant part of the child population is omitted when only married, spouse-present women are studied. In addition, an estimated half of all 1969 patients in family planning programs were never-married or ever-married women not living with a husband. Analysis of program effects on the fertility of women in all marital statuses is therefore necessary to develop a reliable estimate of the program's overall impact.

The first two rows in each panel of Table 6.3 compare mean 1969 SAU fertility rates by race and age based on vital statistics[1] with our 1969 proxy rates—the number of children under one year per 1,000 women in all marital statuses reported by the 1970 census. In the remaining rows of each panel, rates for women in upper and lower socioeconomic subgroups are shown.

Mean SAU vital statistics rates are higher than mean SAU census rates in all but the 30–44 age group, among both whites and blacks. This pattern is expected because some children of younger mothers live with, and are reported to census by, older women (see Appendix A); children under one year living with women 45 and older (or living in a family headed by a man with no female partner) were not included in our analysis. The fact that our proxy rates are generally lower than the actual rates among both whites and blacks is no indication that the proxy rates lack analytic value. They might be compromised if the living arrangements of young children vary systematically so that the children are less likely to live with women aged 15–44 (net of other factors included in analysis of program effects) in areas with higher levels of program enrollment, and if these living arrangement patterns occur only among lower-income, but not upper-income, groups. Without such a systematic pattern, using children under one year per 1,000 women in all marital statuses as the dependent variable probably will not yield biased estimates of program effects.

The center panel of Table 6.3 reports mean fertility rates for whites living in white SAUs. SAUs where whites constituted less than 90 percent of women aged 15–44 in all marital statuses below 200 percent of poverty are excluded

TABLE 6.2

Mean SAU Number of Children Under One Year Living with Women in All Marital Statuses and Married, Spouse-Present Women, by Race and Age: 1970

Marital Status	Age			
	15–44*	15–19	20–29	30–44
White				
All marital statuses	3,716	375	2,589	802
MSP only	3,452	333	2,428	766
Ratio of all to MSP	1.08	1.13	1.07	1.05
Black				
All marital statuses	1,713	306	1,015	411
MSP only	1,127	136	698	293
Ratio of all to MSP	1.52	2.52	1.45	1.40

MSP = married, spouse present.
*Age-specific count need not equal the 15–44 total.
Source: FPP Impact Study.

from these analyses. The mean percent white in "white SAUs" is about 98 percent in all age and economic groups. By this definition all but one teen-age subgroup have 436 white SAUs (see Table 6.4). By physically separating "all-white" SAUs, the measure of program enrollment is not affected by nonwhites, since almost all patients and women of reproductive age in these SAUs are whites. Therefore, the relative level of white compared with nonwhite participation in the program and other factors related to racial heterogeneity of SAUs are controlled. As a result estimates of program effects on white fertility taken from the "white SAU" analyses may be superior to estimates that use all SAUs. White SAU fertility rates are very similar to those for whites in all SAUs.

PROGRAM EFFECTS ON 1969 CHILDREN UNDER ONE YEAR

Table 6.4 summarizes our analyses of program effects on fertility, with the number of SAUs shown to indicate the extent to which all SAUs were or were not included in each equation. Because women in all marital statuses are used, the number of SAUs in each analysis is, with one exception, the total count for the nation when white women living in all SAUs are studied (left third of table). When whites living in white SAUs are examined (center section), the number of SAUs declines with enough left to sustain analyses. Among blacks the coverage of SAUs is high for all subgroups.

TABLE 6.3

Comparison of Fertility Measures Derived from Vital Statistics and 1970 Census, by Age, Race, and SES: 1969

Measure and Type of Group	15–44	15–19	20–29	30–44
White (N = 778)				
Mean SAU vital statistics fertility rate	87	64	163	36
All children under 1 year	81	38	157	41
Children under 1 year below 200% of poverty	110	65	200	61
Children under 1 year above 200% of poverty	66	22	135	31
Children under 1 year below 50% of median income	97	87	155	41
Children under 1 year between 50 and 99% of median income	108	59	186	48
Children under 1 year above 100% of median income	58	12	130	35
White in White SAUs (N = 436)				
Mean SAU vital statistics fertility rate	88	60	168	38
All children under 1 year	83	37	163	43
Children under 1 year below 200% of poverty	111	61	206	65
Children under 1 year above 200% of poverty	67	22	139	32
Children under 1 year below 50% of median income	99	84	159	44
Children under 1 year between 50 and 99% of median income	111	57	193	51
Children under 1 year above 100% of median income	58	12	133	37
Black (N = 237)				
Mean SAU vital statistics fertility rate	116	139	180	48
All children under 1 year	86	64	148	50
Children under 1 year below 200% of poverty	100	71	175	61
Children under 1 year above 200% of poverty	58	43	98	28
Children under 1 year below 50% of median income	102	84	172	56
Children under 1 year between 50 and 99% of median income	89	60	152	51
Children under 1 year above 100% of median income	59	34	101	39

Source: FPP Impact Study.

TABLE 6.4

Summary of Program Enrollment Effects on Children Under One Year per 1,000 Women in All Marital Statuses, by Age, Race, and SES: 1970

Age	White (in all SAUs)			Race and SES — White (in white SAUs)			Black		
	Number of SAUs	Program Enrollment	R^2	Number of SAUs	Program Enrollment	R^2	Number of SAUs	Program Enrollment	R^2
Below 200% of Poverty									
15–44	778	−.014*	.50	436	−.019*	.48	237	−.025*	.44
15–19	778	−.019*	.63	436	−.024*	.63	237	−.026*	.39
20–29	778	−.046*	.55	436	−.057*	.52	237	−.063*	.25
30–44	778	−.019*	.40	436	−.022*	.38	237	−.006	.19
Above 200% of Poverty									
15–44	778	−.003	.64	436	.001	.67	237	−.007	.12
15–19	778	−.004	.44	436	−.010**	.41	187	−.032*	.26
20–29	778	−.025*	.47	436	−.020	.41	237	−.004	.17
30–44	778	−.001	.47	436	.008	.53	235	.005	.07
Under 50% of Median Income									
15–44	778	−.023*	.47	436	−.034*	.45	237	−.024**	.33
15–19	770	−.032*	.49	429	−.050*	.48	225	−.049*	.34
20–29	778	−.036*	.54	436	−.062*	.54	223	−.053*	.19
30–44	778	−.005	.25	436	−.002	.24	234	.013	.28
50–99% of Median Income									
15–44	778	−.025*	.58	436	−.040*	.59	237	−.041*	.34
15–19	778	−.021*	.53	436	−.030*	.57	225	−.010	.39
20–29	778	−.060*	.45	436	−.097*	.36	235	−.062*	.21
30–44	778	−.017*	.34	436	−.013	.37	237	−.027**	.54
Above 100% of Median Income									
15–44	778	−.000	.41	436	.002	.64	236	−.003	.14
15–19	778	−.000	.40	436	−.004	.39	196	−.004	.19
20–29	778	−.021*	.40	436	−.033*	.38	207	−.011	.23
30–44	778	.001	.44	436	.003	.48	216	.013	.08

*$p < .05$.
**$p < .10$.

Notes: "White (in white SAUs)" includes only SAUs in which 90 percent or more of the women aged 15–44 below 200 percent of the federal poverty line were white. Ordinary least-squares regressions, unstandardized coefficients.

Source: FPP Impact Study.

The unstandardized regression coefficient of the program enrollment measure is shown for each race, age, and SES group. These coefficients are from equations including 1969 parity and the standard list of control variables for given age groups. The level of explained variance (R^2) is also shown. Borderline significance is indicated by a double asterisk, while coefficients significant at $p < .05$ and greater than twice their standard error are indicated by a single asterisk.

The decks in the table are specific for SES subgroups. For low-SES white women there are 24 tests of program enrollment (12 in all SAUs and 12 in white SAUs), and 12 more among blacks. Of the 24 tests for low-SES white subgroups, program enrollment has statistically significant negative effects on fertility in 21 equations. Of the 12 tests for low-SES black subgroups, program enrollment has statistically significant negative effects on fertility in seven equations and negative effects of borderline significance in two more. Of the 24 tests involving higher-SES white and black women, program enrollment has a significant negative effect in only one black and three white equations and borderline significance in one other white equation.

When the results in Table 6.4 for women in all marital statuses are compared with those reported in chapter 5 for married women, the patterns are similar: the program shows negative and, in most cases, significant effects depressing the fertility of lower-SES white and black women in all age subgroups. Among higher-SES women program enrollment has few effects that are significant or of borderline significance, except among white women 20–29 years old and teen-agers of both races. The largest coefficients among low-SES whites and blacks are always for 20–29 years old women, who are in their prime childbearing years. In 1969 women aged 20–29 accounted for 67 percent of white and 53 percent of black births.[2] In most cases the coefficients that proved to be significant in the married, spouse-present equations are also significant when women in all marital statuses are studied.

There are two major differences between these results and those reported in chapter 5: First, when women in all marital statuses are studied the coefficients estimating program effects are generally smaller than in the married, spouse-present equations. While this is true for both races, the differences are particularly striking among low-income blacks. Second, when we use the entire population of low-SES teen-agers (rather than only the 8–11 percent who are married and have a spouse present), we have a stable and consistent pattern indicating generally significant program effects that decrease lower-SES teen-age fertility. This is true for both white and black teen-agers. Women under 20 years contributed 15 and 30 percent of total 1969 white and black births, respectively.[3]

In both racial groups women under age 30 contributed more than 80 percent of all 1969 births. Women in these younger age groups, which show the largest absolute program effects on fertility, have constituted an increasing proportion of the patient caseload in the years since 1969. While significant negative effects on the unwanted fertility of subgroups aged 30–44 can be detected, the magnitude of program effects on the older age group often is relatively small. Thus the youthful age of the caseload and the pattern of program enrollment coefficients, by age, may suggest that the program's growth since 1969 should have been accompanied by a further decline in birth planning failures among lower-SES women, especially those under age 30.

We conclude that, independent of other factors, the family planning program in 1969 had a significant negative impact on the fertility of lower-SES white and black women, regardless of the criterion employed to define socioeconomic status and whether we study only married women or women in all marital statuses. The findings are consistent: the higher the proportion of lower SES women estimated to be in need of family planning who are served by the program, the lower will be their fertility. Increases in the number of agencies and locations providing family planning services increase patient caseloads relative to the estimate of need, and higher patient caseloads are a cause of lower fertility. Even in 1969, before the U.S. family planning program experienced its most rapid growth, it helped low-SES women control their fertility more successfully; and this was reflected in lower fertility rates in the subgroups served by the program.

Finally, since analyses of the white SAUs is restricted to those areas in which almost all women of reproductive age and all clinic patients are white, the results may provide more reliable estimates of the program's effects on white fertility than do the results when all SAUs are studied. Accordingly, we utilize the white-SAU coefficients in the next section, where we attempt to determine whether the statistically significant program effects that emerge from this study are of a magnitude that is practically significant as well.

POTENTIAL OF FAMILY PLANNING PROGRAMS TO REDUCE DIFFERENTIAL FERTILITY

The traditional inverse relationship between fertility and SES was documented in chapters 4 and 5. Since fertility studies have shown increasing convergence in family size preferences between socioeconomic groups,[4] reduction or elimination of this historic class differential can be considered one way of expressing the results of a program to provide modern family planning services to women in lower-SES groups. To gauge the practical import of our findings of program effects, we now examine the potential effect of a hypothetical family planning program serving all women in need on differences in the number of children under one year among lower-SES and higher-SES women of both races.

Table 6.5 assembles the information needed for such an assessment. All women of childbearing age are classified in three age groups, and for each age group three comparisons of lower versus higher SES are shown—one in which the classification criterion is the federal poverty index and two in which the criterion is family income alone. Thus, we have nine low-SES versus high-SES comparisons for whites and nine for blacks. In each subgroup the observed mean number of children under one year per 1,000 women is shown, and the low-high differential is computed. These data are followed by the estimated effect on the number of children under one year per 1,000 lower-SES women, net of other factors, of a hypothetical program serving all low-SES women in need of services and having the same impact on the fertility of lower-SES subgroups as the 1969 program demonstrated in our regressions. These are simply the unstandardized regression coefficients of the program enrollment variable from Table 6.4, with the decimal point moved three places to the right. For whites we use the coefficients derived from the studies of predominantly white SAUs. The final line of each cell shows the percent by which the initial class differences in fertility would be reduced by the hypothetical fully implemented program. In this table only statistically significant coefficients are used. It is important to note that these are all period fertility measures, that is, both the class fertility differentials and the estimated fertility reductions induced by the program are rates for a single year in time. The hypothetical program-engendered fertility reductions come from prevention of birth timing as well as number failures. Changes in fertility behavior in one year may result in unpredictable fertility changes in any direction in subsequent years. For example, there is no way of estimating from this model what proportion of timing failures averted as a result of the program would be made up for later, and what proportion would be postponed indefinitely. We cannot predict, in other words, whether class differentials would persist, increase, be further reduced or even be reversed when the various cohorts of women involved have completed their fertility. What the model does illustrate is the direction and something of the magnitude of the program's likely effect on fertility differentials.

Among white teen-agers the estimated number of unwanted births averted by a program enrolling all women in need of services would have eliminated about two-thirds of the initial class differentials in each of the three teen-age low-high comparisons. Virtually all the differences would be removed in the two comparisons that can be made among black teen-agers. The program also had negative effects which were of borderline significance on teenage fertility above the poverty cutoff; as a result the fertility of the higher-SES white and black teen-agers also would be expected to decline with a fully implemented program, and some low-high fertility differential would persist.

Among black women 20–29 years old, the impact of a fully implemented program, net of other factors, would be to eliminate three-quarters or more of the initial fertility differentials (and to reverse them for blacks with 50–99 percent of median income, whose fertility would be lower than that of blacks

TABLE 6.5

Estimates of Potential Effects of Family Planning Programs on Reducing 1969 SES Fertility Differences, by Age, Race, Poverty Status, and Income Group

| | Race and Age | | | | | |
| | White (in white SAUs) | | | Black | | |
	15–19	20–29	30–44	15–19	20–29	30–44
Children < 1 < 200% pov.	61	206	65	71	175	61
Children < 1 > 200% pov.	22*	139	32	43*	98	28
Difference	39	67	33	28	77	33
Estimated program effect	−24	−57	−22	−26	−63	n.s.
Percent difference reduced	62	85	67	93	82	n.r.
Children < 1 < 50% med. inc.	84	159	44	84	172	56
Children < 1 > 100% med. inc.	12	133*	37	34	101	39
Difference	72	26	7	50	71	17
Estimated program effect	−50	−62	n.s.	−49	−53	n.s.
Percent difference reduced	69	238	n.r.	98	75	n.r.
Children < 1 50–99% med. inc.	57	193	51	60	152	51
Children < 1 > 100% med. inc.	12	133*	37	34	101	39
Difference	45	60	14	26	51	12
Estimated program effect	−30	−97	n.s.	n.s.	−62	−27
Percent difference reduced	67	162	n.r.	n.r.	122	225

n.s. = coefficient not significant.

n.r. = not relevant.

*Coefficient for higher-SES group was also significant or of borderline significance.

Note: Expected program effects are based on significant or borderline-significant program enrollment coefficients from Table 6.4.

Source: FPP Impact Study.

above median). Among whites the reductions in the initial class differentials would be even more striking, with the program-induced fertility decline resulting in nearly identical rates for whites below and above the poverty cutoff, and apparently reversing the initial class differences when women are classified by income alone. However, the coefficient of the program enrollment variable was also negative and statistically significant for whites above median income. As a result the fertility of the higher-SES whites aged 20–29 also would decline. The resulting fertility rates, however, would be almost identical for the three subgroups classified by income alone (97 per 1,000 women below 50 percent of median, 96 per 1,000 for those between 50 and 99 percent of median, and 100 per 1,000 women above median income).

Among those 30–44 years old, where 1969 fertility differentials were rather small in absolute terms, we had significant coefficients of program effects in two subgroups. The indicated reduction in the class differential in these subgroups also would be substantial—two-thirds of the higher fertility of whites below the poverty cutoff would be eliminated, while blacks with 50–99 percent of median income would have lower fertility than those with income above the median.

From Table 6.5 we conclude that the program's potential ability to reduce class fertility differences, as measured by 1969 family planning program effects extrapolated to encompass a fully implemented program serving all lower-SES women in need, is large for both whites and blacks in all age groups. It is not necessarily predictive of the magnitude of the program's potential effect on completed cohort fertility.

This finding may be regarded as hypothetical, since it is predicated on the program's achieving 100 percent enrollment of the target population, which is unlikely in any program. The analysis in chapter 3 shows, however, that the proportion of lower-SES women in need who are served by the program can be increased relatively rapidly by increasing the number of agencies and clinic locations providing family planning services. These program activity variables are particularly sensitive to policy change: additional funding can stimulate new agencies to participate in the program and others to expand services at existing locations and to add new locations. Whether or not 100 percent enrollment could realistically be achieved, the effect of a policy to expand the program would be to increase the proportion enrolled and to decrease class differentials in fertility. A second consideration is that the assessment only extrapolates program effects that were measurable in 1969, when only one-seventh of all women in need were served and before the program achieved its most rapid growth. It seems plausible that the program's effects in subsequent years would be greater than are those registered here. More than one-third of lower-SES women in need were enrolled by 1975 and a much larger proportion were young and nulliparous. By reaching more women at a younger age and an earlier stage of family formation, the program should be able to prevent the cycle of continued contraceptive failures typical when a woman begins child-bearing at a relatively young age.[5] In addition, one of the program's main functions has been to introduce modern contraception to persons who used either less effective methods or none at all, and many patients would be likely to continue to use the more effective methods even if they no longer attend family planning clinics (and thus are no longer represented in the patient statistics measuring program enrollment). Thus, we could expect a program to have cumulative effects that would add to those already measurable in its early years.

The fertility of higher-SES groups, of course, also might be changing while the program was being fully implemented, a result of other factors, and an indirect consequence of the program itself (and for some subgroups, such as teen-agers, perhaps as a direct consequence). Some class differentials could well continue even after all lower-SES women in need were served by the program. The main value of the hypothetical data in Table 6.5, in our view, is to document two key conclusions:

1. The program's effects, independent of other factors, on the fertility of lower-SES women in the United States are both statistically and substantively significant. The magnitude of program effects is such as to suggest that the program has the potential to sharply reduce historic class differentials in fertility.

2. Given the fact that family planning programs require few resources, certainly fewer than those required by any of the other factors believed to affect fertility employed in these regressions, a policy to expand rapidly the enrollment of lower-SES persons in family planning clinics would be the most cost-effective means available to reduce class differentials in fertility. It would do so by assisting lower-SES persons to avoid unwanted and mistimed pregnancies that have, in recent years, accounted for most of the remaining class fertility differentials in the United States.

NOTES

1. National Center for Health Statistics, "Final Natality Statistics 1969," *Monthly Vital Statistics Report,* 22 (7): Tables 2 and 4, October 2, 1972. Vital statistics fertility rates that represent mean SAU values tend to be higher than national rates based on individuals. For example, the respective white and black national 1969 fertility rates based on individuals aged 15–44 were 81 and 108, well below our mean SAU rates in Table 6.3.

2. Ibid., Table 2.

3. Ibid.

4. U.S. Bureau of the Census, *Current Population Reports,* Series P.-20, nos. 232 and 277 (Washington, D.C.: U.S. Government Printing Office, 1973 and 1975).

5. N. B. Ryder, "Contraceptive Failure in the United States," *Family Planning Perspectives* 5, 1973, p. 133.

7

SHORT-TERM COSTS AND BENEFITS OF FAMILY PLANNING CLINIC PROGRAMS, 1970-75

The findings of this study can be used in yet another way to gauge the practical effects of the family planning program: they can be extrapolated forward in time to yield estimates of the number of unwanted and unintended births that have been averted through the efforts of organized U.S. family planning clinic programs independent of other social changes. These estimates, coupled with the short-term governmental expenditures that would have been associated with these births had they not been averted, and a comparison of these imputed savings with the federal funds allocated to the family planning program, can be used to compute short-term benefit/cost ratios for the federal funds used in the program—a critical indicator for program analysis and policy making.[1]

Benefit/cost analyses of family planning services are based on the concept that in addition to important health, social, emotional, and demographic benefits, the prevention of an unwanted or unintended birth has two major economic benefits: it avoids the cost of providing for an additional child in the family and it avoids the loss of income by the woman while she is pregnant and while she is rearing the child (or it may enable a woman to take a job to add to the family's income). These benefits accrue both to the individual and to society, and the corollary costs when a birth is not prevented are borne in part by the individual and in part by society in the form of government expenditures.

Benefit/cost analyses have attempted to calculate the long-term benefits of family planning programs by estimating the number of births averted by a program, its costs, and the total expenditures necessary to raise a child to adulthood. These analyses yield a range of long-term benefit/cost ratios, depending on the assumptions employed by the particular investigator. Stephen Enke, for example, who focused primarily on family planning in developing countries, estimated a rate of return of about 100:1.[2] In 1967 Arthur Campbell calculated a long-term benefit/cost ratio of 26:1 for a U.S. family planning program serving low-income persons.[3] In a study in Great Britain, W. A. Laing used a somewhat different approach and estimated long-term benefit/cost ratios for the prevention of specific types of unwanted births: he calculated a ratio of 128:1 for an illegitimate child, 20:1 for a fourth child, and 22:1 for a fifth child.[4]

Some economists have questioned long-term benefit/cost analyses that do not address the issue of the extent to which a child, during his productive years, pays back the cost of his birth and upbringing.[5] Evaluating this issue involves assessment of factors that are difficult to predict, such as the future impact of education and technological change on economic growth in general and, in the context of the U.S. family planning program, on the economic prospects of individuals born today in low-income families.

One of the principal uses of benefit/cost analyses is to assist government officials in making decisions on resource allocation. From their vantage point the issues surrounding long-term benefit/cost studies are not necessarily salient, however significant they may be from a scientific or philosophic point of view. Government decision makers typically function in a limited time frame, bounded on one side by the length of terms of office and on the other by a planning process and methodology in which five years is considered the distant future. Under such conditions decision makers find it difficult to give appropriate weight to the potential claims on public resources, or returns to public resources, that will result two decades in the future from government action or inaction now. Faced with more claims than can be met with the resources at his disposal, the typical official usually evaluates budgetary decisions in terms of their likely impact on government expenditures in the years immediately ahead.

In this chapter, therefore, we seek to answer more limited questions than are posed in long-term benefit/cost studies: Are there savings in government expenditures in year 2 that can be attributed to federal family planning expenditures in year 1? If such savings exist, what is their likely range? The analysis thus concentrates on the short-term costs to government of unwanted and unintended births to women with low or marginal incomes—and, among these, only on costs for which available data make possible a quantified estimate.*

The time period to be analyzed is program years 1970 through 1975, when the number of women served in organized family planning clinics increased

---

*Higher-SES births may also have short-term costs to government, but we have no data with which to quantify them and they are, therefore, excluded from the analysis.

rapidly as federal allocations for the program quadrupled and then leveled off. Both program statistics and expenditure data are reported for fiscal years ending on June 30; our calculations will be done for these time periods, distributing the estimated births averted to the appropriate calendar years in which they would have occurred.

To compute the number of births averted in 1970–75, we utilize the program enrollment coefficients from Table 6.4 and apply them to age-specific and race-specific program statistics for each year. The extrapolation of these coefficients forward in time raises some questions because this study could measure only the effects of the 1968–69 program on period rates of fertility in 1969–70. These effects may be overestimated for some subgroups and underestimated for others, and may be modified by the later fertility behavior of different subgroups. We thus cannot be certain that the effects of the program would remain exactly the same in subsequent years.

On balance, we believe we can appropriately extrapolate these coefficients forward to develop an approximation of the births averted by the program. As noted in Chapter 6, several factors suggest that the magnitude of the program's impact on fertility may have increased since 1969. Not only has the number of patients served by clinics increased from 1.1 million to 3.8 million in this period (Table 1.1), but the clinic caseload has become increasingly younger; by 1975, 30 percent of patients were below age 20, compared with 20 percent in 1969, and 85 percent were below age 30, compared with 78 percent in 1969. The greatest improvement in contraceptive efficacy occurs among these younger patients as a result of clinic enrollment. In 1974 and 1975, for example, more than half the new patients below age 20 used no method prior to enrollment and one-sixth used the less effective methods; at their last clinic visit five-sixths or more of these patients were using pills or IUDs.[6]

The increasingly younger age structure of the caseload implies that the program's role in upgrading the contraceptive practices of women of child-bearing age has increased, not only as a result of the larger number of patients but also because a greater proportion of them are drawn from subgroups that use less effective methods or none at all. The upgrading process should lead directly to fewer timing and number failures, which would be reflected in a greater program impact now than was registered in 1969. Another reason, suggested in chapter 6, is the cumulative effect on the fertility of women who are introduced to effective contraception in a family planning clinic and continue to use it even after they no longer attend the clinic. Finally, contraceptive failure rates probably decline among patients as clinic personnel gain experience, especially in dealing with teen-age patients. As a result of these trends, using the 1969 coefficients may yield estimates that understate both the program's effects on fertility in subsequent years and the estimates of births averted. Resolving these questions would require that the study be replicated for a later time, which is not possible because of the unavailability of adequate small-area data. In any case, these coefficients provide a more reliable means than has heretofore been available to estimate the number of births averted as a result of the program.

BIRTHS AVERTED, 1970–75

The procedures used to estimate the number of low-income and marginal-income births averted by the program, net of other factors, from 1970 through 1975 are shown in Appendix Table C.1. For each year, and for each age and race subgroup, the number of women served by the program was obtained, the number in need of family planning estimated, and the ratios of patients served to estimated need calculated. These ratios, measuring the proportion of the estimated need in each subgroup served in each year, correspond to the program enrollment variable used in the multiple-regression equations in this study (except that in 1969 the measure could not be specified by age and race).* The ratios are multiplied by the appropriate program enrollment coefficient from Table 6.4 to yield the estimated number of births averted per 1,000 women in the subgroup.† Multiplication of this number by the estimated number of women in the subgroup results in an estimate of the total number of subgroup births averted that are attributable to the program in each year.

Table 7.1 summarizes these calculations. As a result of the patients served in the six years from fiscal 1970 through fiscal 1975, an estimated 1.1 million low-income and marginal-income births were averted—767,000 among white women and 330,000 among blacks. Nearly two-thirds of these averted births were a result of patients served in the last half of the period.

These estimates provide an approximate measure of the program's impact during a six-year period, independent of other factors, on the fertility of women with incomes below twice the poverty index. Our regression equations also yielded a statistically significant program activity coefficient among black teen-agers above 200 percent of poverty, and a coefficient of borderline significance among white teen-agers in that SES subgroup. Using procedures identical with those applied to low-income and marginal-income women, we derived

---

*We are indebted to Joy G. Dryfoos of the Alan Guttmacher Institute for these computations, as well as for assistance in obtaining cost data for public assistance and medical and social services.

†In the calculation of white births averted, we use the program activity coefficients derived from the analyses of women in white SAUs in Table 6.4, since nearly all patients and women in need in these SAUs are white and the measurement of program enrollment among whites is not vulnerable to errors resulting from differential enrollment of nonwhite and white patients in racially mixed SAUs. Superior measurement of white program participation rates should result in better estimates of program effects on white fertility.

TABLE 7.1

Estimated Low-Income and Marginal-Income Births Averted by Family Planning Clinic Programs: 1970-75

Fiscal Year in Which Patients Were Served	Estimated Births Averted		
	Total	White	Black
1970	96,472	66,483	29,989
1971	131,592	91,813	39,779
1972	178,010	121,661	56,349
1973	203,054	140,890	62,164
1974	218,578	154,177	64,401
1975	269,890	192,351	77,539
Total	1,097,596	767,375	330,221

Source: Appendix Table C.1.

an estimated 266,000 averted births among teen-agers above 200 percent of poverty in 1970–75—226,810 among whites and 38,784 among blacks (see Appendix Table C.2). These estimates are not included in calculations of benefit/cost ratios below.

These are, of course, estimates of the program's direct effects only, since we have no means of quantifying its indirect effects on the family planning practices and success in regulating fertility of persons not served by the program.

SHORT-TERM GOVERNMENTAL COSTS SAVED BY AVERTING UNWANTED AND UNINTENDED BIRTHS

Our estimates of the short-term costs to government of low-income and marginal-income births are significantly understated by the paucity of available data. With readily available information, estimates are possible only for the following types of costs:

- Medical care associated with pregnancy and birth (prenatal care, delivery, and postpartum care for the mother, and care of the infant for the first year of life). For low-income and marginal-income women a significant part of these costs is currently borne by federal, state, and local government through Medicaid, special health projects, and tax-supported hospitals and health centers.
- Public assistance during the first year for children born to women already on public assistance.

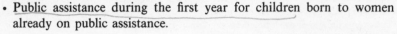

· Selected social services for public assistance recipients and their newborn for one year.

That these do not exhaust even the short-term governmental costs associated with low-income and marginal-income births must be emphasized. At least four exclusions demonstrate that these estimates seriously understate the short-term costs.

1. Some women and their infants would become public assistance recipients as a result of the birth.

2. Some low-income and marginal-income persons who are not public assistance recipients do participate in other public programs, such as food stamps, social services, and public housing, which are included in these estimates for public assistance recipients only.

3. Both public assistance recipients and other low-income and marginal-income persons participate in other public programs, such as child welfare, and antipoverty efforts, which are omitted entirely from these estimates.

4. Some women experience opportunity costs of income lost due to the need to give up employment during pregnancy and the early period of rearing a child. These costs are reflected in reduced family income, and may in turn generate increased government expenditures for additional social, health, and housing services.

These categories are excluded from the estimates because information is not available with which to specify the proportion of low-income and marginal-income women who fall into each category and the resulting amounts of governmental expenditure. The omitted costs to government are considerable; if they could be specified, the short-term savings per birth averted that are estimated below could possibly double.* Rather than engage in speculation on these issues, however, we prefer to carry out an analysis based on available documented costs, which, though understated, are likely to be beyond dispute.

The data and procedures used to calculate the costs of medical care, public assistance, and related services per low-income and marginal-income

---

*The opportunity cost per low-income and marginal-income birth averted in 1971 was estimated at $1,044; if half were a cost to government, the estimated governmental savings per birth averted at that time (see F. S. Jaffe, "Short term costs and benefits of United States family planning programs," *Studies in Family Planning,* 5: Table 7 and 102–03, 1974) would have increased by more than 80 percent. In subsequent years expenditures for food stamps, social services, and other public programs have increased significantly and the costs associated with nonwelfare participants in these programs are omitted from this analysis, as are the costs of public programs for which even the extent of welfare participants is unknown.

birth averted are detailed in Appendix D. Table 7.2 summarizes the estimates of governmental expenditures for maternity and first-year pediatric care per low-income and marginal-income birth in 1970–75; included are the costs of hospitalization and of physicians' services for normal deliveries as well as the added costs for premature infants, Caesarean births, congenital anomalies, and sick infants. The cost per birth to government has increased from an estimated $489 in 1970 to $1,021 in 1975, partly as a result of the rapid escalation in medical care costs and partly because the governmental share has increased from half of total costs to nearly 69 percent.*

The estimated average national cost of cash assistance, social services, food stamps, and public housing per public assistance recipient ranges from $792 in 1970 to $1,353 in 1975 (Table 7.3). Of all patients of family planning clinics in the years under study, the proportion receiving public assistance ranged from 16 to 19 percent. We assume that the proportion of births averted by family planning programs that would have occurred to public assistance recipients is at least the same as their proportion in the caseload. Based on this assumption, the estimated saving in governmental expenditures for cash assistance and these selected services per birth averted among all family planning patients ranges from $151 in 1970 to $217 in 1975.

In Table 7.4 the estimates of savings in medical care, public assistance, and selected services are summed to a total estimate of savings in governmental expenditure per birth averted by the family planning clinic program. The savings increase from $640 per birth averted in 1970 to $1,238 in 1975.

FEDERAL EXPENDITURES FOR FAMILY PLANNING SERVICES AND BENEFIT/COST RATIOS

We are now able to estimate the ratio of benefits to government from these short-term savings to the cost to the federal government of the family planning program. To do this it is necessary to determine the federal expenditures applicable to each year's savings. Federal funds for family planning service projects typically have been awarded in the last quarter of one fiscal year to be used in the following fiscal year. The time lag between a grant award, delivery of family planning services, and a birth averted is therefore at least nine months. Funds awarded at the end of fiscal 1969 (May–June 1969), for

---

*These estimates may well understate the current actual costs. Compared with our 1975 estimate of $1,491 for the total cost of maternity care and first-year pediatric care including complications, for example, the costs of maternity care alone for normal delivery in New York City in 1976 are estimated at about $1,200 for hospitalization and $500–$700 for physicians' services. See "Staggering expenses of having a baby," New York *Times,* January 23, 1976, p. 37.

TABLE 7.2

Approximations of Governmental Expenditures for Medical
Services per Low-Income and Marginal-Income Birth: 1970-75
(In dollars)

Year	Total Cost of Hospital and Physicians' Services (1)	Governmental Expenditures			
		Hospital Services (2)	Physicians' Services (3)	Total (4 = 2+3)	Percent of Total (5 = 4÷1)
1970	961	395	93	488	50.8
1971	1,062	473	115	588	55.4
1972	1,121	505	142	647	57.7
1973	1,169	545	171	716	61.2
1974	1,289	609	218	827	64.2
1975	1,491	735	286	1,021	68.5

Source: Appendix tables D.1, D.2, D.3.

example, were used for services between July 1969 and June 1970; their impact
on births began to be reflected in April 1970, and continued throughout
calendar 1970 and into the first quarter of 1971. The appropriate relationship,
therefore, is between fiscal 1969 grants and births averted between April 1970
and March 1971. The benefit/cost ratios for federal family planning expenditures, based on this time lag, are shown in Table 7.5.

From fiscal 1969 through fiscal 1975, the federal government appropriated $584 million in grants for family planning projects.* The minimum
estimated savings to government in medical care, public assistance, and social
service costs in each single year following these expenditures total, for the six
years, nearly $1.1 billion. The short-term benefit/cost ratio over the period was

---

*The federal expenditures shown include only funds awarded under project and formula
grant authorizations for family planning projects, because these funds are the principal sources
of support for family planning clinics and our program enrollment coefficients measure the effects
of services delivered by clinics alone. Omitted from the expenditure data are reimbursement
programs such as Medicaid and social services; these programs have published no reliable information about family planning expenditures, but insofar as they have paid for family planning services,
they have financed primarily services delivered by physicians in private practice. Our coefficients,
of course, do not measure the impact of such services. To the extent that these programs may have
financed some clinic services (particularly after 1973), the federal expenditures reported here are
understated and the resulting benefit/cost ratios are overstated.

TABLE 7.3

Estimated Governmental Expenditures for Public Assistance and Selected Services per Birth Averted: 1970–1975

	1970	1971	1972	1973	1974	1975
1. Total average annual cost of public assistance and selected services (social services, food stamps, other food programs, and public housing) per AFDC recipient ($)	792	885	1,028	1,108	1,281	1,353
2. Proportion of family planning clinic patients receiving public assistance (%)	19	18	17	17	16	16
3. Costs of public assistance and selected services per 100 births averted ($) (1x2)	15,048	15,930	17,476	18,836	20,496	21,648
4. Estimated savings in public assistance and selected services per birth averted ($) (3÷100)	150.48	159.30	174.76	188.36	204.96	216.48

Source: Item 1, from Appendix Table D.4; Item 2, data for 1971–75 from National Reporting System for Family Planning Services; 1970 figure estimated.

TABLE 7.4

Estimated Savings in Governmental Expenditures per Birth Averted by Family Planning Clinic Programs: 1970-75
(In dollars)

Year	Total Savings $(1 = 2+3)$	Governmental Expenditures	
		Hospital and Physicians' Services[a] (2)	Public Ass't. and Selected Services[b] (3)
1970	639	488	151
1971	747	588	159
1972	822	647	175
1973	904	716	188
1974	1,032	827	205
1975	1,238	1,021	217

Sources: Column 4 from Table 7.2; Row 4 from Table 7.3.
[a]From Table 7.2;
[b]From Table 7.3.

1.8:1; a dollar invested by the federal government in family planning in one year saved federal, state, and local governments a minimum of $1.80 a year later.*

As noted above, the framework for this analysis is extremely limited and undoubtedly underestimates even the short-term savings to government that accrue as a result of family planning services for low-income and marginal-income persons. Nevertheless, the short-term return to public funds alone during the 1970s has been high, without taking into consideration the economic, social, health, and personal benefits to the individuals and families. Few, if any, public programs in the United States have the potential of saving a minimum of nearly two dollars in government expenditures in Year 2 for every dollar expended in Year 1. A noteworthy fact is that the bulk of these first-year savings derive from the costs of medical care associated with pregnancy; only about one-fifth derive from the cost of public assistance.

---

*These benefit/cost ratios apply to the federal investment in organized family planning services, not to total public and private expenditures for these services. Federal outlays have both financed the cost of services directly and stimulated investment of other funds in family planning by state and local government, private philanthropy, and, in some cases, partial fees paid by patients. Systematic data are unavailable on the extent of financing through these nonfederal sources; a reasonable guess would be that nonfederal funds amounted to less than 20 percent of the federal investment between 1970 and 1975. The addition of these nonfederal funds on the cost side would reduce somewhat the ratios of return presented here.

TABLE 7.5
Computation of Estimated Short-Term Cost/Benefit Ratios of Federal Expenditures for Family Planning Clinic Programs: 1970–75

Calendar Year When Births Were Averted	Births Averted[a] (1,000) (1)	Saving per Birth Averted (2)	Total Estimated Savings ($ million) (3 = 1 × 2)	Fiscal Year of Appropriation (4)	Federal Appropriations for Family Planning Clinic Services ($ millions)[d] (5)	Benefit/ Cost Ratio (6 = 3 ÷ 5)
1970	72.4[b]	639	46.3	1969	32.8	1.4:1
1971	122.8	747	91.7	1970	51.9	1.8:1
1972	166.4	822	136.8	1971	73.3	1.9:1
1973	196.8	904	177.9	1972	136.9	1.3:1
1974	214.7	1,032	221.6	1973	129.7	1.7:1
1975	324.5[c]	1,238	401.7	1974	159.7[e]	2.5:1
Total	1,097.6		1,076.0		584.3	1.8:1

Notes: The computation assumes that savings are proportional to births, in the absence of any information on economies of scale or of utilization of a fixed capacity for services. Totals computed before rounding.

[a]The estimated number of births averted (from Table 7.1) attributable to services provided during a fiscal year (ending June 30), distributed 75 percent to same calendar year and 25 percent to next calendar year; for instance, 96,472 births were averted by services provided in fiscal year 1970, 72,354 of which would have occured during 1970 and 24,118 of which would have occured during the first quarter of 1971.

[b]Omits an estimated 18,000 births averted as a result of services provided in fiscal year 1969.

[c]Includes 67,000 averted births attributable to services provided in fiscal year 1975 that would have occurred in calendar year 1976.

[d]Includes appropriations for project and formula grants under Title X of the Public Health Service Act, Title V of the Social Security Act, and, in earlier years, Title II of the Economic Opportunity Act. Omitted are expenditures under Medicaid (Title XIX of the Social Security Act), and social services programs (Titles IV-A and XX of the Social Security Act), and other third-party reimbursement programs that publish no reliable information on family planning expenditures; insofar as these programs have paid for family planning services, they primarily finance services delivered by physicians in private practice, rather than by clinics. To the extent that Titles IV-A, XIX, and XX have financed clinic services, the federal expenditures reported here are understated and the resulting benefit/cost ratios overstated. See J. G. Dryfoos, "A National Family Planning Program: The U.S. Experience 1968–1974," *Studies in Family Planning*, Table 13: April 1976, for estimates based on information from DHEW and Alan Guttmacher Institute.

[e]Includes $30 million in impounded funds appropriated in fiscal 1973 that were released in fiscal 1974 for nonrecurring expenditures only.

These savings are in addition to the long-term savings—and the health, social, and demographic benefits to government and individuals—from the prevention of unwanted and unintended births. The government resources saved as a result of family planning programs would in principle be freed to finance other urgent health and social needs in the year following the program expenditure.

NOTES

1. This chapter adapts the methodology used in F. S. Jaffe, "Short term costs and benefits of United States family planning programs," *Studies in Family Planning,* 5:98, March 1974. That article, however, employed arbitrary assumptions about the number of births averted as a result of program enrollment, while this analysis utilizes the program effects documented in this study.

2. S. Enke, "The economic aspects of slowing population growth," *Economic Journal,* March 1966.

3. A. A. Campbell, "The role of family planning in the reduction of poverty," *Journal of Marriage and the Family,* 30:236, May 1968.

4. W. A. Laing, *The Costs and Benefits of Family Planning* (London: Political and Economic Planning, 1972).

5. See, for example, H. Leibenstein, "Pitfalls in benefit/cost analysis of birth prevention," *Population Studies,* 23:161, July 1969.

6. Data on age characteristics and contraceptive methods of patients in 1974 and 1975 are from Alan Guttmacher Institute, *Data and Analyses for 1975 Revision of DHEW Five-Year Plan for Family Planning Services* (New York: Alan Guttmacher Institute, 1975); and *Data and Analyses for 1976 Revision of DHEW Five-Year Plan for Family Planning Services* (New York: Alan Guttmacher Institute, 1976).

8

CONCLUSIONS AND
POLICY IMPLICATIONS

CONCLUSIONS

The primary goal of this study has been to test the hypothesis that U.S. family planning programs reduce unwanted fertility among subgroups from which clinic patients are drawn.* To test this hypothesis we rely on 1970 census reports of the number of children under one year living with women of reproductive age because only census fertility data are specific to income and poverty status. In contrast, vital statistics natality data cannot be specified to the socioeconomic groups from which family planning clinic patients are drawn.

Defining and measuring program effects on fertility can be done in several ways. The best way, of course, would be to measure the fertility of individuals before and after they enrolled in the program, compared with a control group of comparable persons who are not enrolled. Measuring the fertility of subgroups of women by area was necessary, however, because of data limitations. Our approach allows a direct test of the effect on annual fertility rates of an

---

*A program will not decrease unplanned pregnancy unless it reduces the contraceptive failure rate of patients after as compared with before, they enter the program.

For example, it can be shown that in a subgroup of women with a 50 percent annual failure rate before enrolling in the program, all of whom enroll in the program, and had a 10 percent failure rate as patients, their rate of unplanned pregnancies will be reduced by 80 percent. See P. Cutright, "Illegitimacy in the United States—1920-68", in C. F. Westoff and R. Parks (eds.) *Social and Demographic Determinants of Population Growth,* vol. 1, U.S. Commission on Population Growth and the American Future, *Commission Research Reports* (Washington, D.C.: U.S. Government Printing Office, 1972) Table 34.

area's having few or many patients enrolled in clinic programs, per 1,000 women below 200 percent of poverty who are estimated to be in need of family planning services. Measurement of this program effect occupies most of chapters 5 and 6. An alternative approach to the study of program effects on fertility, discussed in chapter 4, takes a longer view of the effects of past organized efforts in an area to improve family planning delivery systems. The principal conclusion from this discussion that is relevant to this study's primary goal is that the effect of the past must be adequately controlled before the program's effect on an annual rate can be accurately measured.

The study divides the white and black female population within counties into age, marital, and socioeconomic subgroups. The county is the building block for geographic areas called SAUs. Counties with few white or black women aged 15-44 are combined with contiguous counties until a minimum population size is reached. A limit was set that would provide enough white or black women in each subgroup for statistical analysis of their fertility rates. SAUs used to examine effects on white fertility have 20,000 or more white women aged 15-44, while "black" SAUs have 10,000 or more black women aged 15-44. The difference in size is related to differences in the poverty status distributions of the two populations.

We examine alternative ways to use the detailed information on white and black women by age, marital status, and SES in SAUs to provide the best estimates of program effects on the number of children under one year in the population subgroups served by the program, net of other factors believed to affect fertility. After certain checks were made (and given the relatively small number of SAUs with high proportions of women in need actually served by the program in 1969), we chose to rely on ordinary least-squares multiple-regression analysis rather than multiple-classification analysis. The problem was not so much with selection of the proper multivariate method as with the development of a research design and statistical controls that would allow adequate testing for program effects on 1969 fertility rates.

Basically, we rely on a weight of evidence approach, although, looking backward, the data now seem so clear-cut that such an approach appears unduly cautious. Nevertheless, the weight of evidence approach is appropriate because the measure of program enrollment is not specific to subgroups; the maximum theoretical effects on fertility of a program in which all women in need were served are often very small, and detecting program effects is difficult in some groups (such as older women).

This design relies on multiple control groups and compares all possible subgroups of women classified by age, race, marital status, and SES. Thus, for any subgroup the equation assessing the effects of program enrollment on fertility of women below the poverty cutoff (and in the population served by the program) is tested on the fertility of women of the same race, age, and marital status above the cutoff. If the program, rather than other factors, affects fertility, consistent negative and significant program effects should be found among those below the cutoff, while the groups above the cutoff should not have such effects. These multiple comparisons establish whether an increase in the number of patients served per 1,000 women in need below 200 percent of poverty in an area is a cause of levels of fertility lower than those a comparable group of women would have experienced in the absence of an organized program or in an area with a program serving proportionately fewer women in need.

Because we want a measure of program effects that is not contaminated by possible relationships with other factors that affect fertility, we include in equations estimating program effects a number of sociodemographic variables believed to influence fertility: age structure, population density, educational attainment, migration rates, marital status, school enrollment, and labor force participation. In most cases our measures of these variables are specific to each age, race, marital status, and SES subgroup in each SAU. To control factors affecting fertility not captured by these independent variables and to control for effects of prior levels of program development, we include as an independent variable a measure of the subgroup's fertility prior to the time when program effects on the annual fertility rate are being studied. To this list of independent variables we add our measure of program enrollment—the number of patients in organized programs in 1969 per 1,000 women in need below 200 percent of poverty.

The program enrollment measure is not specific to age, race, or marital status but is specific to each SAU. Possible problems in using such an imperfect measure are discussed chapter 2, and we conclude that the measure should be used without attempting any adjustments. As a result, the program effect on some subgroups is underestimated and is overestimated for others. In chapter 4 this model is tested on vital statistics data and CEB. Those tests, in turn, provide evidence of long-run program and community effects on cumulative fertility rates.

Before proceeding with the analysis of program effects on children under one year, we analyzed the determinants of the proportion of low-SES women in need who were served by organized family planning programs in 1969 and in 1971. This analysis shows that the demographic, socioeconomic, or health care characteristics of communities do not determine the proportion served, although they do have small effects. The most important determinant is the level of program activity, as measured by the number of clinic locations and agencies involved in providing services to low-SES women in need. The proportion of women in need served can be raised rapidly by increasing the number of agencies and clinic locations providing family planning services. These program activity variables are particularly sensitive to policy change: additional funding can rapidly induce new agencies to participate and others to provide additional services at existing clinics and to set up new clinics.

The effects of program enrollment on children under one year for white and black wives aged 15-44, 20-29, and 30-44, using two criteria for socioeconomic classification, are summarized in Table 5.7. The level of program enrollment (the number of patients served per 1,000 women in need below 200 percent of poverty) has a negative impact on the fertility of lower-SES subgroups of all ages and both races, and is statistically significant in 18 of 21 comparisons. In contrast, program enrollment is unrelated to fertility in 14 of 15 subgroups of upper-SES wives.

There are relatively few teen-age wives, and this group is examined separately. Among whites program enrollment has a negative and significant effect on fertility of teen-age wives with family incomes between 50 and 99 percent of U.S. median income, while the coefficient for white teen-agers under 50 percent of median income is negative but not significant (Table 5.10). For black teen-age wives the most stable coefficients are estimated for all wives regardless of SES (family income analysis could not be run because of the small black SAU sample size). Among these wives the program enrollment measure took the largest standardized (and negative) coefficient for children under one year with a p value of .12, suggesting a program impact on this teen-age married group as well (Table 5.11).

The plausibility of these estimates of program effects on marital fertility is tested by extrapolating the results based on 1969 data to a hypothetical program serving all women in need. Comparing the estimated impact of such a program on low-SES wives by race and age with 1970 NFS estimates of the proportion of births among these subgroups during 1968–70 that were planning failures, we find no instance in which our estimated reductions in fertility would be greater than what wives told NFS interviewers they would prefer to have experienced (Tables 5.12 and 5.13).

When we turn to women in all marital statuses in chapter 6, we find a similar consistent pattern of strong program effects primarily in the subgroups served by the program. The level of program enrollment has a negative impact on the fertility of women in all lower-SES subgroups and is statistically significant ($p < .05$) in 28 of 36 comparisons and only slightly less significant ($p < .10$) in two others. In contrast, program enrollment is unrelated to fertility in 19 of 24 tests involving subgroups of upper-SES women (Table 6.4). Under rigorous statistical controls, the weight of the evidence thus shows that the larger the proportion of lower SES women enrolled in clinic programs, the lower their fertility.

These significant program effects demonstrate a genuine need for organized family planning services even in an industrialized nation like the United States: if no need existed, there could be no program effects. They also imply that what has been described as the "substitution effect"—that the program serves women who otherwise would have obtained equally effective contraception in the private sector—is a spurious issue in the United States. What the program has done is to enable large numbers of lower-SES women to "substi-tute" more effective medical contraceptive methods for less effective nonmedi-cal methods, and thus to improve their ability to avoid unwanted and unintended conceptions.

Statistical significance does not always indicate practical significance. To gauge the meaning of the statistically significant program effects shown in our equations, we extrapolated the coefficients in different ways to suggest the magnitude of the potential reduction in fertility implied by our findings. When we extrapolate the coefficients to estimate the effect of a hypothetical program that serves all low-income and marginal-income women in need, we find that two-thirds to five-sixths of the initial differences in fertility between white women in the three age groups (15-19, 20-29, and 30-44) below and above 200 percent of poverty would be reduced as a result of the program, net of other factors. Among blacks 82 percent of the difference in fertility by poverty level would be reduced among those 20-29 years old and 93 percent among those 15-19 years old. A comparable analysis compares white and black women above and below median income and yields similar results.

Net of other factors, a fully implemented voluntary program could thus greatly reduce, or in some cases eliminate entirely, historic class differences in fertility in the United States among both white and black women (Table 6.5). Since the program probably would never be fully implemented, the main value of this hypothetical extrapolation is to provide a means of understanding the substantive significance of the statistically significant coefficients of program effects shown in our regressions. It also demonstrates that a policy to increase the proportion of low-SES women in need who are enrolled in clinic programs is a policy to reduce class differentials in fertility. The policy would achieve this result by assisting lower-SES women to avoid unwanted and unintended births.

In chapter 7, our findings are extrapolated forward to provide approxima-tions of the number of births averted by family planning clinic programs between 1970 and 1975. On the basis of age-specific and race-specific program statistics for those years and the program enrollment coefficients that emerge from this study, clinic programs, net of other factors, assisted low-income and marginal-income women of both races to avert an estimated 1.1 million un-wanted or mistimed births (Table 7.1) and higher-SES teen-agers to avert an estimated 266,000 births. The costs to government of a very limited set of selected services associated with the 1.1 million low-income and marginal-income births—maternity and pediatric care for the first year of life and public assistance, social services, and public housing for one year for women already on welfare—are estimated, as are the costs to the federal government of support for family planning clinic programs. These estimates show that fed-eral, state, and local governments saved a minimum of nearly $1.1 billion in the costs of these limited services as a result of the low-income and marginal-income births averted in 1970–75, compared with federal appropriation of $584 million for family planning projects (Table 7.5). For 1970–75 the short-term benefit/cost ratio of family planning clinic programs is 1.8:1—one dollar expended by the federal government on the program in year 1 returned at least $1.80 in governmental savings as a result of births averted in year 2. Although the estimates of births averted and governmental costs associated with low-income and marginal-income births are believed to be understated, few, if any, public programs in the United States have the potential to yield this level of immediate return to public investment. These savings are in addition to the long-term savings—and the health, social, and demographic benefits to society and to individuals—that accrue from the prevention of unwanted and unintended births.

POLICY IMPLICATIONS

These findings confirm the expectations underlying the federal policy, beginning in the mid-1960s that made possible the rapid growth of family planning clinic services. At the same time they raise serious questions regarding the change in policy in 1973 that reduced the federal commitment to the program and cut its annual rate of growth by nearly two-thirds.

The development of an affirmative U.S. public policy on family planning, beginning with the issuance in 1966 of the Department of Health, Education and Welfare's (DHEW) first policy statement on the subject, is described elsewhere.[1] The change was predicated on a set of expectations regarding the behavior of low-income and marginal-income persons that originated primarily in the findings of the 1955 and 1960 Growth of American Families Studies[2] and the 1965 NFS.[3] In broad outline these studies showed that low-income and marginal-income wives desired about the same number of children as higher-income wives and that most had used or expected to use some form of fertility control. However, they had more unwanted and mistimed births than higher-income wives did and, therefore, continued to have higher fertility rates. The studies also showed that a larger proportion of poorer than of higher-income wives relied on the less effective nonmedical birth control methods.

Accordingly, the affirmative public policy on family planning was grounded on the major premises that if effective medical methods were made available and accessible, low-income and marginal-income persons would (1) utilize the services to improve their fertility control practices and (2) as a result would reduce their incidence of unwanted and unintended pregnancy. To make these methods available and accessible required, in program terms, the participation of agencies willing to provide physician-based fertility control services to persons who had only limited access to physicians in private practice for most forms of health care. The federal government's principal policy instrument to obtain this kind of cooperation from the health system is the project grant, which is authorized and appropriated to be given only to those agencies willing to carry out the purposes of the program.

As a consequence of the policy change and subsequent congressional actions, federal appropriations for family planning projects increased significantly in the late 1960s and early 1970s. Hundreds of local health agencies—hospitals, health departments, and voluntary organizations—were stimulated to initiate clinic programs. Between fiscal 1968 and fiscal 1973, the number of health agencies providing family planning clinic services increased from about 1,800 to 3,250, a gain of nearly 80 percent; and the number of counties with family planning clinic locations increased from 1,200 to 1,904.[4] This rapid growth was spurred almost entirely by the initiative of the federal government, with little or no assistance from the states.

The response of low-income and marginal-income persons to the availability and accessibility of medical family planning services followed exactly the predictions of the premises underlying the policy: the number of clinic patients increased from 540,000 in 1966 to 3.8 million in 1975 (Table 1.1). These patient statistics were available from the annual reports on the program issued by DHEW, but they left unanswered the question of whether the program was having the expected effect on fertility. The findings of this study confirm the validity of the policy's second major premise: not only were the services rapidly utilized, but the program has significantly reduced unwanted and unintended fertility among subgroups from whom clinic patients are drawn, demonstrated here under extensive statistical controls.

The development of federal policy reached a high point in 1970 with the passage of the Family Planning Services and Population Research Act. As a result federal appropriations for family planning projects nearly doubled in fiscal 1972, the year in which the program experienced its peak growth. In compliance with this act, DHEW prepared and submitted to Congress in 1971 a five-year plan outlining a program to service all low-SES women in need of family planning services by 1975.[5] This objective was not achieved. A major reason was that in 1973 the federal government abandoned its commitment to the national program goal, even though the national goal had been articulated by the president in 1969.

The switch in federal policy on family planning was an integral part of the philosophy of "new federalism," which has sought to reduce or eliminate direct federal involvement in human service programs. The "new federalist" initiative was justified by the broad allegation that the social programs of the 1960s had "failed" to achieve their objectives. Although the family planning program was demonstrably succeeding, its project grant appropriation was nevertheless frozen at the fiscal year 1972 level and, except for the impounded funds released during fiscal 1974, it has remained at approximately this level in a period of acute inflation (Table 7.5).

The abandonment of the federal commitment to the program was masked to some degree by the other part of the "new federalist" philosophy, which rationalized the reduction of federal involvement in service programs on the ground that such programs should more appropriately be the responsibility of the states. In 1973 a DHEW spokesman, testifying in opposition to renewal of the family planning program's authorizing legislation, expressed the department's position that the financing of family planning services should henceforth be a responsibility of the states, not the federal government:

> The individual state plans will determine the goals and priorities for family planning services within each of the states and the aggregate of these goals and priorities will constitute the national program. . . . We strongly oppose the . . . continued proliferation of unnecessarily categorical authorizations. . . . We believe that direct federal funding of family planning services should no longer be expanded.[6]

But it was specifically the direct federal funding of family planning projects, beginning in 1965, that had brought about a rapid increase in the availability of family planning services and their utilization by low-income and marginal-income persons. State governments generally had shown little interest in allocating their funds to these services and had developed little capacity to administer the program; even in fiscal 1974, after some state and local governments had begun to provide support for family planning, state and local government funds still accounted for only 7 percent of total expenditures for family planning clinic services throughout the nation.[7] To expect the states to take over the primary responsibility for financing and administering the family planning program was plainly unrealistic. Expecting that all 50 states would give equal priority to family planning was equally unrealistic, even if a few states could be expected to take major responsibility for the program. The "new federalism" thus implicitly accepted continuation of wide disparities in availability of services between states. Although its principal formulators have left government service, their policy has continued to dominate the approach of the executive branch toward human service programs.

The results of this reversal of federal policy are discernible in Table 1.1: between 1972 and 1975 the program achieved an average annual rate of increase in patients served of only 13 percent, compared with an average annual rate of growth of 32 percent between 1968 and 1972, when federal appropriations increased rapidly. The findings of this study help to explain this drastic shift: the freeze in federal project grant appropriations since 1972 has meant that fewer new agencies have been induced to provide family planning services and fewer existing provider agencies have been able to open clinics at new locations or expand their services in other ways. As chapter 3 demonstrates, these program activity variables are the principal determinants of increased caseloads.

The "new federalist" initiative was a wide-ranging effort, as one observer put it, "to change national priorities ... [with] sweeping reductions in the domestic expenditures of the federal government, including elimination or sharp curtailment of many programs ... [and] major revisions in the way the federal government deals with state and local governments."[8] The family planning program, which accounted for less than one-twentieth of one percent of the federal budget, probably did not loom very large in the considerations underlying this policy. Yet the program was not spared the consequence of the effort to reduce the federal presence.

The major consequence, simply put, is that a smaller proportion of low-income and marginal-income women in need of family planning services receive them today than would have received them had the federal government stood by its commitment to the program. As this study has shown, low-income and marginal-income women therefore continue to have unwanted and unintended births that could have been avoided by more available and accessible voluntary family planning services; and federal, state, and local governments continue to spend significant amounts for medical and social services for these births.

In this light any policy to reduce the federal commitment to the family planning program and transfer responsibility for it to state and local government constitutes a policy to maintain class fertility differentials in the United States for a longer time than would be the case had the federal government continued to assign priority to the program. This probably was not the result intended by the authors of current federal policy, but it was the result nonetheless. This study has shown that rapidly reducing these differentials is entirely feasible if the federal commitment to a national priority effort can be revived and the program's momentum restored.

NOTES

1. F. S. Jaffe, "Public policy on fertility control," *Scientific American,* 229 (1):17, July 1973.

2. R. Freedman, P. K. Whelpton, and A. A. Campbell, *Family Planning, Sterility and Population Growth* (New York: McGraw-Hill, 1959); and P. K. Whelpton, A. A. Campbell, and J. Patterson, *Fertility and Family Planning in the United States* (Princeton, N.J.: Princeton University Press, 1966).

3. N. B. Ryder and C. F. Westoff, *Reproduction in the United States, 1965* (Princeton, N.J.: Princeton University Press, 1971). For a discussion of the relationship between these fertility studies and the U.S. public family planning program, see F. S. Jaffe, "Knowledge, perception and change: notes on a fragment of social history," *Mt. Sinai Journal of Medicine,* 42:286, July/August, 1975; and O. Harkavy, F. S. Jaffe, and S. M. Wishik, "Family planning and public policy: who is misleading whom?" *Science,* 165:367, July 25, 1969.

4. Fiscal 1968 data from Office of Economic Opportunity, *Need for Subsidized Family Planning Services: United States, Each State and County, 1968* (Washington, D.C.: U.S. Government Printing Office, 1969); fiscal 1973 data from Center for Family Planning Program Development, *Data and Analyses for 1974 Revision of DHEW Five-Year Plan for Family Planning Services* (New York: Center for Family Planning Program Development, 1974).

5. Senate Committee on Labor and Public Welfare, *Report of the Secretary of Health, Education and Welfare Submitting Five-Year Plan for Family Planning Services and Population Research Programs* (Washington, D.C.: U.S. Government Printing Office, 1971).

6. Testimony of H. E. Simmons, M. D., deputy assistant secretary of the Department of Health, Education and Welfare on May 8, 1973, in Senate Committee on Labor and Public Welfare, *Family Planning Services and Population Research Amendments of 1973,* 93rd Congress, First Session, pp. 47–48, 55.

7. D. Lewis, J. MacKenzie, R. B. Nestor, and B. Shprecher, "Expenditures for organized family planning services in the United States: 1974," *Family Planning Perspectives* 8:39, January/February 1976.

8. K. Gordon, in introduction to E. R. Fried, A. M. Rivlin, C. L. Schultze, and N. H. Teeters, *Setting National Priorities: The 1974 Budget* (Washington, D.C.: Brookings Institution, 1973), p. vii.

DO DIFFERENCES IN MEASURES
OF MARITAL FERTILITY
AFFECT ESTIMATES OF PROGRAM EFFECTS?

In this appendix we first compare mean SAU marital fertility rates (MFR) based on vital statistics data with the number of children under one year per 1,000 wives, derived from the 1970 census, used to estimate program effects on marital fertility. Both rates use the same denominator: the number of spouse-present wives. The numerator of the vital statistics rate is the count of legitimate births in SAUs in which 90 percent or more of births to women of a given age and race were coded by legitimacy status.* The numerator of the census measure is children under one year living in a household with a spouse-present wife. The identical set of SAUs is used in the following analysis. The means and standard deviations of measures used in this analysis are slightly different from those for married, spouse-present women in the main body of the study because some SAUs do not report the legitimacy status of children. About 80 percent of white and 84 percent of black SAUs are retained.

THE RATIO OF MFR TO CHILDREN UNDER ONE YEAR

Table A.1 shows the MFR and the rate of children under one year by race and age of wife. MFR is always larger than the rate of children under one. The magnitude of this difference is measured by the ratio of MFR to children under one, shown in the third row of each panel. We would expect this ratio to be greater than 1.0 because (1) infant mortality decreases the number of children under one, (2) any legitimate birth to a woman who is not married, spouse-present, and aged 15–44 will be excluded from the census measure, and (3) the

---

*California and Georgia natality statistics were deleted from the NCHS data for analyses by legitimacy because those states do not report legitimacy to NCHS. From the public health departments of these states, county-level counts of legitimate and illegitimate births, by race and age of mother, were obtained. California data are for 1970 rather than 1969, because of the concern expressed by California authorities about the reliability of county-level 1969 data on legitimate births. Georgia data are for 1969. The addition of these two states added 68 SAUs to the total number of SAUs available for analysis of whites, and also increased coverage of black SAUs. In counties reporting the legitimacy of 90 percent or more of total births, the illegitimacy ratio (illegitimate births per 1,000 total births with legitimacy indicated) was calculated. This ratio was applied to the total count of births in the SAU, which gave an adjusted count of illegitimate births. Subtracting adjusted illegitimate births from total births yields an adjusted count of legitimate births. Legitimate births divided by the number of 1970 married, spouse-present women is a proxy for the 1969 MFR. The rate is specific to race and age.

MFR may be inflated by misreporting of legitimacy, although this probably is not an important cause of the differences shown in Table A.1. It is more difficult to misreport an illegitimate birth as legitimate than is commonly recognized.[1] If the census undercount of children under one year is greater than census undercount of married, spouse-present women, this also will inflate the ratio.

Because the living arrangements of white and black legitimate children are different, we would expect higher ratios among blacks than whites.[2] From R. R. Rindfuss we expect the ratio to be highest among teen-agers, lower among women 20–29, and, in the case of whites, below 1.0 for women 30–44.[3] Rindfuss refers to this change in the ratio over age groups in terms of a transference of the children of young "biological" mothers to older "sociological" mothers. Our data conform to the expected pattern within racial groups by age, and follow the expected difference in level of the ratio by race.

TABLE A.1
Marital Fertility and Ratio of MFR to Children Under One Year per 1,000 Wives, by Age and Race: 1970

		Race			
		White		Black	
Age	Measure	Mean	S. D.	Mean	S. D.
15–44	MFR	126	28	181	34
	Children under one year	115	13	133	21
	Ratio	1.100	.21	1.371	.21
	Number of SAU's	620		199	
15–19	MFR	482	168	676	150
	Children under one year	282	54	368	69
	Ratio	1.760	.73	1.893	.52
	Number of SAU's	591		82	
20–29	MFR	214	48	277	53
	Children under one year	199	24	208	31
	Ratio	1.076	.22	1.345	.26
	Number of SAU's	618		199	
30–44	MFR	41	12	65	20
	Children under one year	44	10	60	18
	Ratio	.922	.17	1.132	.35
	Number of SAU's	579		200	

Source: FFP impact study.

THE EFFECT OF INFANT MORTALITY

In this set of SAUs the mean 1969 infant mortality rates were 16.8 infant deaths per 1,000 vital statistics births among whites and 37.4 among blacks. To adjust the 1969 MFR for infant mortality, the infant mortality rate is multiplied by the 1969 MFR for women 15–44 and divided by 1,000. This yields 2.1 for whites and 6.7 for blacks. Subtracting these numbers from the 1969 MFR yields an MFR that is reduced for infant deaths and thus is conceptually more comparable with the census rate. However, the adjustment has only a small effect on the ratios in Table A.1. For women 15–44 the white ratio declines to 1.08 and the black ratio to 1.31. We conclude that infant mortality is not an adequate explanation of the fact that the ratios of the two rates differ from 1.00. Nor does infant mortality account for much of the difference between racial groups.

DO DIFFERENCES IN THE RATIO OF MFR TO CHILDREN UNDER ONE YEAR BIAS ESTIMATES OF PROGRAM EFFECTS ON CHILDREN UNDER ONE YEAR?

If the ratio of MFR to children under one year varied among SAUs because the accuracy of the census count of children under one year varied, then it is possible that SAUs with high patient caseloads were more or less likely to suffer census undercount than SAUs with few patients. Under these conditions the program enrollment measure would take a spurious and negative relationship to children under one year.* In Table A.2 we test the possibility that the program enrollment variable is significantly related to the ratio of MFR to children under one year when the same variables in the analysis of program effects are used to predict variation among SAUs in the MFR/children under one year ratio.†

In Table A.2 we find no significant relationship for any race or age group between our measure of program enrollment and the ratio under study. None of these coefficients achieve even borderline significance. Moreover, the low level of explained variance suggests little correlation between any of the variables used in these equations and variation among SAUs on this dependent variable. We conclude that real differences in the level of marital fertility, as

---

*This effect would be unlikely if, as seems plausible, one or more of the other variables in the equations we use to estimate program impact were more highly correlated to census undercount (or to other factors affecting the count of children under one year) than program enrollment.

†This is not a test of the census undercount effect alone, but of whether any factors affecting the ratio are related to the program enrollment measure.

TABLE A.2
Effects of Program Enrollment on Ratio of MFR to Children Under One Year per 1,000 Wives, by Age and Race: 1970

Age	Measure	Race White	Race Black
15–44	Program enrollment	.057	- .017
	R^2	.089	.040
	Number of SAU's	620	199
15–19	Program enrollment	.043	.065
	R^2	.050	.058
	Number of SAU's	591	82
20–29	Program enrollment	.054	.036
	R^2	.067	.051
	Number of SAU's	618	199
30–44	Program enrollment	.017	- .073
	R^2	.059	.077
	Number of SAU's	579	200

Notes: Figures are for SAU's reporting legitimacy of births. The coefficient for program enrollment is the coefficient in the equation used to measure program effects. That equation includes program enrollment, age 20–29 (for women 15–44), low education, migration, never married, in school (except for the 30–44 age group), labor force, and parity 1969. Ordinary least-squares regressions, standardized coefficients.

Source: FFP impact study.

measured by the MFR and our measure of children under one year, are unrelated to the measure of program enrollment and, therefore, it is unlikely that estimates of program effects within age and race groups are biased.

NOTES

1. See P. Cutright, "Illegitimacy in the United States:1920–68," in C. F. Westoff and R. Parke, Jr., eds., *Social and Demographic Determinants of Population Growth,* vol. I of U.S. Commission on Population Growth and the American Future, *Commission Research Reports,* Washington, D.C.: U.S. Government Printing Office, 1972), App. A.

2. J. Sweet, "The family living arrangements of children," working paper 74–28 (Madison: University of Wisconsin, Center for Demography and Ecology, 1974), Table 3. The data in Sweet's report are from the 1967 Survey of Economic Opportunity.

3. R. R. Rindfuss, "Annual fertility rates from Census data: method, assumptions, and limitations," working paper 74–21 (Madison: University of Wisconsin, Center for Demography and Ecology, 1974), Tables 3–5.

Data on birth planning failures by age and race for 1968–70 births to married, spouse-present women were provided by Charles F. Westoff and Lois Paul of Princeton from the 1970 NFS. Two types of failures are shown in Tables B.1 and B.2. Timing failures generally represent births that the couples would have preferred to occur at a later time, while number failures represent births that were not wanted at any time. Because these figures refer to births, they understate the extent of birth planning failures because they omit induced and spontaneous fetal loss to couples trying to space or prevent additional births.[1] They tell us the proportion of total births during the 1968–70 period that were defined as planning failures by married, spouse-present wives, classified by race, age, income, and poverty status.

Because a family planning program can only reduce number and timing failures, the degree to which the program can be viewed as achieving its goal can be assessed by its effects on unwanted and mistimed births. The 1970 NFS data defined wives by race and age groups compatible with our classifications. However, their poverty definition is at 150 percent of the federal poverty index, rather than the 200 percent cutoff we use. Therefore, in order to use these NFS estimates to gauge the extent to which the 1969 organized family planning program showed a potential for meeting its goal of reducing unwanted and mistimed births among low-income and marginal-income wives, we adjusted the birth planning failure data to fit our 200 percent of poverty cutoff.

There is no clear-cut procedure to get "one best estimate" of the proportion of births to married, spouse-present women in the interval between 150 and 200 percent of poverty that were birth planning failures. Inspection of Table B.1 shows that for whites, poverty status among wives with family income in the $5,000–$9,999 interval is related to the reported incidence of unplanned births. Because virtually all births to women with family income under $5,000 were to those below 150 percent of poverty, while all births to women with family income over $10,000 were to those above 150 percent of poverty, the only comparisons "controlling income" between the incidence of unplanned births and poverty status are restricted to women in the income range of $5,000–$9,999. Since it appears likely that wives within this income range defined as below or above 200 percent of poverty differ by family size, a difference in the incidence of unplanned births by poverty status is expected.

An upward bias would be apparent if one assumed that the incidence of unplanned births among women between 150 and 200 percent of poverty is the same as it is among those below 150 percent of poverty. This seems clear, in Tables B.1 and B.2, from the comparisons of failure rates reported by wives in the $5,000–$9,999 range below and above 150 percent of poverty. Therefore,

TABLE B.1
Proportion of 1968–70 Births to White Wives, Defined as Number and Timing Failures, by Age, Poverty Status, and Income Group

Age	Poverty Status	Family Income			
		Under $5,000	$5,000–$9,999	$10,000 or More	Total
Proportion Number Failures					
15–44	All wives	.079	.106	.127	.114
	Below 150% of poverty	.080	.283	*	.196
	Above 150% of poverty	*	.053	.127	.095
30–44	All wives	.316	.302	.255	.273
	Below 150% of poverty	.316	.426	*	.402
	Above 150% of poverty	*	.183	.255	.240
20–29	All wives	.049	.071	.068	.068
	Below 150% of poverty	.049	.203	*	.131
	Above 150% of poverty	*	.040	.068	.057
Under 20	All wives	.000	.000	.055	.011
	Below 150% of poverty	.000	*	*	.000
	Above 150% of poverty	*	.000	.055	.014
Proportion Timing Failures					
15–44	All wives	.371	.284	.258	.278
	Below 150% of poverty	.380	.239	*	.299
	Above 150% of poverty	*	.297	.258	.274
30–44	All wives	.158	.237	.194	.207
	Below 150% of poverty	.158	.176	*	.172
	Above 150% of poverty	*	.296	.194	.216
20–29	All wives	.402	.283	.284	.293
	Below 150% of poverty	.406	.257	*	.327
	Above 150% of poverty	*	.289	.284	.286
Under 20	All wives	.421	.411	.389	.409
	Below 150% of poverty	.471	*	*	.550
	Above 150% of poverty	*	.377	.389	.370

131

TABLE B.1 (Continued)

Age	Poverty Status	Family Income			Total
		Under $5,000	$5,000–$9,999	$10,000 or More	
All Failures Combined					
15–44	All wives	.450	.390	.385	.392
	Below 150% of poverty	.460	.522	*	.495
	Above 150% of poverty	*	.351	.385	.369
30–44	All wives	.474	.540	.449	.480
	Below 150% of poverty	.474	.603	*	.575
	Above 150% of poverty	*	.479	.449	.455
20–29	All wives	.451	.354	.352	.361
	Below 150% of poverty	.455	.460	*	.458
	Above 150% of poverty	*	.329	.352	.343
Under 20	All wives	.421	.411	.444	.419
	Below 150% of poverty	.471	*	*	.550
	Above 150% of poverty	*	.377	.444	.384
Number of Births					
15–44	All wives	140	803	827	1,770
	Below 150% of poverty	137	184	0	321
	Above 150% of poverty	3	619	827	1,449
30–44	All wives	19	139	263	421
	Below 150% of poverty	19	68	0	87
	Above 150% of poverty	0	71	263	334
20–29	All wives	102	608	546	1,256
	Below 150% of poverty	101	113	0	214
	Above 150% of poverty	1	495	546	1,042
Under 20	All wives	19	56	18	93
	Below 150% of poverty	17	3	0	20
	Above 150% of poverty	2	53	18	73

*Proportion of failures not computed when the number of births was 10 or fewer.
Source: 1970 National Fertility Study.

TABLE B.2

Proportion of 1968–70 Births to Black Wives, Defined as Number and Timing Failures, by Age, Poverty Status, and Income Group

Age	Poverty Status	Family Income			
		Under $5,000	$5,000–$9,999	$10,000 or More	Total
Proportion Number Failures					
15–44	All wives	.342	.264	.167	.247
	Below 150% of poverty	.342	.478	*	.429
	Above 150% of poverty	*	.131	.167	.147
30–44	All wives	.467	.529	.304	.444
	Below 150% of poverty	.467	.560	*	.525
	Above 150% of poverty	*	*	.304	.344
20–29	All wives	.300	.235	.117	.205
	Below 150% of poverty	.300	.429	*	.387
	Above 150% of poverty	*	.123	.117	.120
Under 20	All wives	*	.040	*	.034
	Below 150% of poverty	*	*	*	*
	Above 150% of poverty	*	.040	*	.038
Proportion Timing Failures					
15–44	All wives	.237	.345	.262	.307
	Below 150% of poverty	.237	.194	*	.209
	Above 150% of poverty	*	.439	.261	.361
30–44	All wives	.067	.206	.043	.125
	Below 150% of poverty	.067	.160	*	.125
	Above 150% of poverty	*	*	.043	.125
20–29	All wives	.300	.348	.333	.338
	Below 150% of poverty	.300	.214	*	.242
	Above 150% of poverty	*	.425	.333	.383
Under 20	All wives	*	.520	*	.552
	Below 150% of poverty	*	.520	*	.538
	Above 150% of poverty	*			

TABLE B.2   (Continued)

Age	Poverty Status	Under $5,000	$5,000–$9,999	Family Income $10,000 or More	Total
All Failures Combined					
15-44	All wives	.579	.609	.428	.554
	Below 150% of poverty	.579	.672	*	.638
	Above 150% of poverty	*	.572	.428	.508
30-44	All wives	.533	.735	.348	.569
	Below 150% of poverty	.533	.720	*	.650
	Above 150% of poverty	*	*	.348	.469
20-29	All wives	.600	.583	.450	.544
	Below 150% of poverty	.600	.643	*	.629
	Above 150% of poverty	*	.548	.450	.504
Under 20	All wives	*	.560	*	.586
	Below 150% of poverty	*	*	*	*
	Above 150% of poverty	*	.560	*	.577
Number of Births					
15-44	All wives	38	174	84	296
	Below 150% of poverty	38	67	0	105
	Above 150% of poverty	0	107	84	191
30-44	All wives	15	34	23	72
	Below 150% of poverty	15	25	0	40
	Above 150% of poverty	0	9	23	32
20-29	All wives	20	115	60	195
	Below 150% of poverty	20	42	0	62
	Above 150% of poverty	0	73	60	133
Under 20	All wives	3	25	1	29
	Below 150% of poverty	3	0	0	3
	Above 150% of poverty	0	25	1	26

*Proportion of failures not computed when the number of births was 10 or fewer.
Source: 1970 National Fertility Study.

to avoid overestimating the incidence of unwanted births among all women below 200 percent of the poverty cutoff, we used an estimating procedure based on these 1970 NFS data.

To illustrate the method of estimating the proportion of 1968–70 births to wives below 200 percent of poverty that were planning failures, we take the example of white wives aged 30–44. In this age group we have (Table B.1) the number of births to women below 150 percent of poverty (87) and the proportion of these births reported as birth planning failures (.575). For the same wives we have an additional 71 births to women in the $5,000–$9,999 income interval above 150 percent of poverty, .479 of which were defined as birth planning failures. We have a total of 158 births to white women in the under-$10,000 family income interval. About 55 percent of the 158 total births were to women below 150 percent of poverty, and 45 percent to those above 150 percent of poverty. The sum of the two products provided by the proportion of births in the given category and the proportion of planning failures in the

TABLE B.3
Adjusted Proportion of 1968-70 Births Defined as Planning Failures by Wives Below 200 Percent of Poverty, by Race and Age

Poverty Level	Age			
	15–44	15–19	20–29	30–44
White				
Under 150% poverty	.495	.550	.458	.575
Under 200% poverty	.400	.425	.368	.532
Number of births*	940	73	709	158
Black				
Under 150% poverty	.637	.586	.629	.650
Under 200% poverty	.605	.563	.585	.665
Number of Births*	212	28	135	49

*Number of 1968-70 births to NFS wives under 150 percent of poverty plus births to wives above 150 percent of poverty in the $5,000-$9,999 family income interval.

Source: 1970 National Fertility Study.

category equals a weighted estimate of planning failures to wives with family income below $10,000 in 1969. We use these estimates to approximate failures to wives below the 200 percent of poverty cutoff used to define women in need.

As indicated in Table B.3, these estimates are slightly lower than would have been used had the adjustment process not been followed. Given differences in the incidence of birth planning failures among wives below and above poverty, the lower failure rates estimated by the adjustment procedure for women under the 200 percent level seem reasonable and were applied to estimates of the impact of organized family planning programs on controlling unwanted fertility among low-income and marginal-income married couples in the United States in chapter 5.

NOTES

1. P. Cutright, "Spontaneous fetal loss: a note on rates and some implications" *Journal of Biosocial Science,* 7:421, November 1975.

APPENDIX C
BIRTHS AVERTED BY FAMILY PLANNING
CLINIC PROGRAMS: 1970-75

The coefficients of the program enrollment variable in Table 6.4 provide a straightforward means to estimate the number of births averted by family planning clinic programs, independent of other factors affecting fertility, in subsequent years. The program enrollment variable is the ratio of the number of women served by the program per 1,000 women below 200 percent of poverty who are estimated to be in need of family planning services. All that is necessary in order to use the coefficients to estimate the effects of the program in a given year is to compute these ratios for the year under study. Use of the coefficients in this manner implies the assumption that the magnitude of program effects after 1969 was the same as that found for 1969. As discussed in chapter 7, the program impact may have been greater in 1970–75 than in 1969; but the question could be answered satisfactorily only by replicating the study for a later period, which is not possible because of data limitations. The program enrollment coefficients provide a better means than has heretofore been available to estimate births averted, but the resulting estimates should be regarded as approximations.

Table C.1 assembles the information needed to estimate the number of averted births among low-income and marginal-income women that would have occurred had there been no family planning clinic program between 1970 and 1975.* The reporting period for federal programs is the fiscal year, from July 1 through June 30. Assuming that the intake of patients is uniform during a program year, services provided by the program during a fiscal year could begin to affect births by the following April 1. This time lag is used in chapter 7 to allocate the estimated births averted as a result of services rendered during a given fiscal year to the appropriate calendar years when governmental expenditures would have occurred if the births had not been averted.

The age-specific and race-specific patient statistics presented in column 1 of Table C.1 are derived from DHEW's National Reporting System for Family Planning Services for fiscal 1971–75; for fiscal 1970 they are estimated from the total number of patients served and fragmentary reports on their characteristics. The number of women below 200 percent of poverty in each age and race subgroup (column 6) is derived from special tabulations of the Census Bureau's Current Population Surveys for 1970, 1972, 1974, and 1975, and

---

*Age-specific and race-specific data for 1970–75 on patients served, women estimated to be in need of service, and total number of women in each subgroup were computed by J. G. Dryfoos of the Alan Guttmacher Institute.

TABLE C.1

Calculation of Estimated Low-Income and Marginal-Income Births Averted by Family Planning Clinic Programs, by Race and Age: 1970-75

Program Year (fiscal) and Age	Total Patients in Organized Programs (1,000) (1)	Estimated Women < 200% of Poverty in Need of Family Planning Services (1,000) (2)	Program Enrollment Variable (ratio of patients to women in need) (3 = 1 ÷ 2)	Program Enrollment Coefficient (4)	Estimated Births Averted per 1,000 Women (5 = 3 × 4)	Number of Women < 200% of Poverty (1,000) (6)	Estimated Births Averted by Program (7 = 5 × 6)
White							
1970							
15-19	209	761	.2746	-.024	6.59	2,597	17,115
20-29	518	2,504	.2068	-.057	11.79	3,651	43,037
30-44	160	2,283	.0700	-.022	1.54	4,111	6,331
Total	887	5,548	.1599			10,359	66,483
1971							
15-19	344	771	.4461	-.024	10.71	2,628	28,136
20-29	684	2,706	.2527	-.057	14.40	3,954	56,953
30-44	172	2,437	.0705	-.022	1.55	4,335	6,724
Total	1,200	5,914	.2029			10,917	91,813
1972							
15-19	463	803	.5765	-.024	13.84	2,754	38,104
20-29	922	2,932	.3144	-.057	17.92	4,151	74,389
30-44	242	2,559	.0945	-.022	2.08	4,410	9,168
Total	1,627	6,294	.2585			11,315	121,661
1973							
15-19	587	805	.7291	-.024	17.50	2,601	45,513
20-29	1,114	2,937	.3792	-.057	21.61	3,967	85,744
30-44	273	2,485	.1098	-.022	2.42	3,988	9,633
Total	1,974	6,227	.3170			10,556	140,890
1974							
15-19	640	766	.8355	-.024	20.05	2,448	49,087
20-29	1,190	2,710	.4391	-.057	25.03	3,782	94,659
30-44	290	2,180	.1330	-.022	2.93	3,565	10,431
Total	2,120	5,656	.3748			9,795	154,177

(continued)

1975							
15-19	739	757	.9762	-.024	23.43	2,514	58,900
20-29	1,387	2,736	.5069	-.057	28.89	4,147	119,821
30-44	337	2,174	.1550	-.022	3.41	3,997	13,630
Total	2,463	5,667	.4346			10,658	192,351
1970-1975 Total							
15-19							236,855
20-29							474,603
30-44							55,917
Total							767,375
Black							
1970							
15-19	121	516	.2344	-.026	6.09	922	5,619
20-29	294	891	.3299	-.063	20.78	1,122	23,319
30-44	108	800	.1350	-.006	0.81	1,298	1,051
Total	523	2,207	.2370			3,342	29,989
1971							
15-19	174	550	.3163	-.026	8.22	979	8,051
20-29	385	933	.4126	-.063	25.99	1,172	30,465
30-44	130	814	.1597	-.006	0.96	1,318	1,263
Total	689	2,297	.3000			3,469	39,779
1972							
15-19	255	579	.4404	-.026	11.45	1,035	11,851
20-29	537	970	.5536	-.063	34.88	1,222	42,619
30-44	193	824	.2342	-.006	1.41	1,337	1,879
Total	985	2,373	.4151			3,594	56,349
1973							
15-19	307	593	.5177	-.026	13.46	1,040	13,999
20-29	597	990	.6030	-.063	37.99	1,214	46,119
30-44	211	831	.2539	-.006	1.52	1,343	2,046
Total	1,115	2,414	.4619			3,597	62,164
1974							
15-19	342	596	.5738	-.026	14.92	1,044	15,575
20-29	614	996	.6164	-.063	38.83	1,206	46,833
30-44	206	837	.2461	-.006	1.48	1,350	1,993
Total	1,162	2,429	.4784			3,600	64,401

(continued)

(Table C.1 continued)

Program Year (fiscal) and Age	Total Patients in Organized Programs (1,000) (1)	Estimated Women < 200% of Poverty in Need of Family Planning Services (1,000) (2)	Program Enrollment Variable (ratio of patients to women in need) (3 = 1 ÷ 2)	Program Enrollment Coefficient (4)	Estimated Births Averted per 1,000 Women (5 = 3 × 4)	Number of Women < 200% of Poverty (1,000) (6)	Estimated Births Averted by Program (7 = 5 × 6)
1975							
15–19	404	610	.6622	–.026	17.22	1,083	18,646
20–29	714	1,043	.6845	–.063	43.12	1,314	56,664
30–44	232	838	.2768	–.006	1.66	1,342	2,229
Total	1,350	2,491	.5420			3,739	77,539
1970–1975 Total							
15–19							73,741
20–29							246,019
30–44							10,461
Total							330,221

Sources: col. 1 from National Reporting System for Family Planning Services for 1971-75, racial distribution estimated for 1970; cols. 2 and 6 derived from Current Population Surveys for 1970, 1972, 1974, and 1975, adjusted as in J.G. Dryfoos, "A formula for 1970: estimating the need for subsidized family planning services in the U.S.," *Family Planning Perspectives*, 5:145, Summer 1973; col. 4 from Table 6.4.

TABLE C.2
Calculation of Estimated Births Averted by Family Planning Clinic Programs Among Teen-Agers Above 200 Percent of Poverty, by Race: 1970-75

Program Year (fiscal)	Program Enrollment Variable (1)	Program Enrollment Coeff. (2)	Estimated Births Averted per 1,000 Women (3 = 1 × 2)	Number of Women 15-19 > 200% (4)	Estimated Births Averted by Program (5 = 3 × 4)
White 15-19					
1970	.2745	−.010	2.75	5,409	14,853
1971	.4461	−.010	4.46	5,489	24,486
1972	.5765	−.010	5.77	5,568	32,100
1973	.7291	−.010	7.29	5,919	43,155
1974	.8355	−.010	8.36	6,271	52,394
1975	.9762	−.010	9.76	6,128	59,822
Total					226,810
Black 15-19					
1970	.2344	−.032	7.50	357	2,678
1971	.3163	−.032	10.12	382	3,866
1972	.4404	−.032	14.09	406	5,722
1973	.5177	−.032	16.57	447	7,405
1974	.5738	−.032	18.36	487	8,942
1975	.6622	−.032	21.19	480	10,171
Total					38,784

Sources: Col. 1 from Table C.1, Col. 3; Col. 2 from Table 6.4.

from projections based on these data for 1971 and 1973. Estimates of need for family planning services in each age and race subgroup (column 2) are obtained by adjusting the total number of women in the subgroup to deduct those who are not at risk of unwanted pregnancy—those who are sexually inactive, sterile, pregnant, or seeking pregnancy; these estimates are computed by utilizing the same procedures as those used to compute the comparable estimates for fiscal 1969 that served as the denominator of the program enrollment variable in the regressions in this study.[1]

In column 3 the ratios of patients served to estimated need are presented for each program year; they correspond to the program enrollment measure used in our equations (except that for 1969 the measure could not be specified by age and race). The program's growth from 1970 to 1975 is indicated by the change in this measure—from 160 patients per 1,000 white women in need in 1970 to 435 in 1975, and from 237 per 1,000 black women in need in 1970 to 542.*

Column 5 presents the coefficients from Table 6.4 of the negative effects of the 1969 program on 1970 fertility among low-income and marginal-income women; for whites the coefficients used are those from analyses of white SAUs, since almost all patients and women in need of services in these SAUs had to be white. These are the unstandardized coefficients that show the net direct effect of a change of one unit in the program enrollment variable on the dependent variable measuring children under one year per 1,000 women in each subgroup. Multiplication of the ratios of patients to need (column 4) by the program effect coefficients (column 5) thus yields the number of births averted per 1,000 women in each subgroup (column 6). This figure in turn is multiplied by the number of women in each subgroup to obtain the number of births averted as a result of the delivery of services to low-income and marginal-income women in family planning clinics, independent of other social, economic, and cultural factors believed to affect fertility.

As discussed in the text, the coefficients employed in this computation may understate program effects for some subgroups and overstate them for others because of imperfections in the variable measuring 1969 program enrollment. Nevertheless, the resulting estimates of births averted can be regarded as moderate estimates of the program's direct effects on low-income and marginal-income fertility between 1970 and 1975.

The coefficients of program effects measure only the program's direct effects and omit the indirect effects on fertility of those not served by the

---

*These ratios are higher than are currently reported elsewhere because the need estimates used are based on the formula used in J. Dryfoos, "A formula for the 1970s: estimating need for subsidized family planning services in the U.S.," *Family Planning Perspectives,* 5:145, Summer 1973.

program. Moreover, as noted above and discussed in chapter 7, we expect that the magnitude of the direct effects has increased since 1969.

Finally, it is important to note that these are births averted that are attributable to the family planning services provided to low-income and marginal-income women by clinics only. Some low-income and marginal-income women received family planning services from physicians in private practice, and some of these services may be financed through public programs such as Medicaid. The number in this category is unknown, however, and the program enrollment variable employed in our regressions measures reported patients of organized clinics only.

An estimate of nearly 1.1 million low-income and marginal-income births averted is shown in Table C.1—767,000 among whites and 330,000 among blacks. In addition to program effects on low-income and marginal-income fertility, Table 6.4 shows a statistically significant program effect on the fertility of black teen-agers above 200 percent of poverty, and an effect of borderline significance on white teen-age fertility in this SES group. Using procedures identical to those employed in Table C.1, the number of births averted among higher-SES white and black teen-agers is estimated in Table C.2. For the six years under study, the total is 266,000—227,000 among whites and 39,000 among blacks. Since a significant number of higher-SES teen-agers receive services at family planning clinics, these births averted can appropriately be attributed to the program, although we make no attempt in chapter 7 to estimate the resulting savings in governmental expenditures.

NOTE

1. The estimating procedure is reported in J. G. Dryfoos, "A formula for the 1970s: estimating need for subsidized family planning services in the U.S.," *Family Planning Perspectives,* 5:145, Summer 1973. The estimates in column 2 differ from estimates published in 1975, when the estimating procedure was revised to incorporate later information on increased sexual activity among unmarried persons, a higher incidence of sterility among married couples, and a greater proportion of additional marital childbearing intended within five years; the effect of these modifications was to increase the proportions of unmarried persons at risk of unwanted pregnancy and thus to increase the number estimated to need family planning services. These adjustments are reported in J. G. Dryfoos, "Women who need and receive family planning services: estimates at mid-decade," *Family Planning Perspectives,* 7:142, July/August 1975. Since the coefficients of program effects in this study derive from equations in which estimates based on the earlier formula were used, the earlier formula is the appropriate one to use in extrapolating program effects from 1970 to 1975.

APPENDIX D
SHORT-TERM COSTS OF MEDICAL CARE, PUBLIC ASSISTANCE, AND SOCIAL SERVICES ASSOCIATED WITH LOW-INCOME AND MARGINAL-INCOME BIRTHS: 1970-75

The short-term costs associated with low-income and marginal-income births employed in this analysis are restricted to medical care of the mother during pregnancy and delivery, and of the newborn for the first year of life; public assistance costs for children born to women already on welfare; and costs of selected social services for public assistance recipients and their newborn for the first year of life. Data sources and estimating procedures are described in this Appendix.

MEDICAL COSTS

The medical services directly associated with childbirth are those related to maternity and to care of the newborn during the first year; in addition to normal deliveries and the sick-baby and well-baby care of normal infants, the services include the care for complications associated with pregnancy, for fetal loss, and for premature infants and those with congenital anomalies. In previous studies, estimates of the proportion of births in each of these statuses, and of the costs of maternity and pediatric care for each of these conditions in 1970–71, were derived from the most recent national data reported by government agencies and professional organizations.[1] The available data are not ideal for purposes of this analysis for two reasons: They cover different reporting periods, and they do not clearly delineate costs to government as distinguished from third-party payers or the individuals themselves. Despite these limitations, however, estimates were made that represented approximately the costs of delivery and infant care in 1970–71. These totaled $889 if the birth occurred in a public hospital and $1,134 if it occurred in a voluntary hospital; about 73 percent of these costs covered hospitalization of the mother and the infant, while the remainder covered physicians' services during pregnancy and the infant's first year. The estimates omitted medical costs for institutional and home care of retarded infants and utilized a national incidence rate for congenital abnormalities, rather than a rate specific for lower socioeconomic groups. For these reasons the estimate was regarded as understating the true costs.

For purposes of this analysis, we assume that half of the women below 200 percent of poverty deliver their babies in public hospitals and half in voluntary hospitals. We therefore take as our starting point the average of the estimated public and voluntary hospital costs—$1,011—as representing the average total cost of maternity and first-year pediatric care of a low-income or marginal-income birth in 1970–71. Adjusted by the medical care components of the Consumer Price Index (CPI) the total comes to $961 in 1970 and $1,062 in 1971.

Table D.1 adjusts these costs to take account of the inflation in medical prices since 1970, using the separate components of the CPI for physicians' fees and hospital costs. By 1975 the total average cost had increased to $1,491.

Not all these costs are borne by government; some are paid by the individuals or through health insurance. Only fragmentary information is available on the share of these costs borne by government. Government expenditures for hospital care that may be applicable to maternity and pediatric care can be isolated by using data published by the Social Security Administration. These computations are shown in Table D.2. For example, of the total of $18 billion spent by government in 1972 for hospital care, $10.4 billion was allocated through programs that do not generally include maternity and pediatric care (such as Medicare, Veterans Administration, vocational rehabilitation, and workmen's compensation). The remaining programs—public assistance vendor payments, general hospital and medical care, and maternal and child health—spent $7.6 billion, which constituted the maximum total government expenditure that could be applicable to maternity and pediatric care.

American Hospital Association statistics show that maternity admissions constituted 9.7 percent of all hospital admissions. Applying this proportion to the total of $7.6 billion yields a gross approximation of $740 million as the amount that federal, state, and local governments could have expended for maternity services in 1972. Women in families with incomes below twice the poverty level (who include most, if not all, potential recipients of subsidized care) had about 1,466,000 births in 1972 with an average total hospital cost of $790 per birth; the estimated total expended was thus $1,158.2 million. Crudely estimated, the government's share of these costs was about 64 percent. Similar computations for each year yield the estimated governmental share of total hospital costs per low-income and marginal-income birth shown in the bottom row of Table D.2, which increases from $395 in 1970 to $735 in 1975.

A comparable analysis of the available data is presented in Table D.3 to arrive at an approximation of the governmental share of the costs of physicians' services. This cost per low-income and marginal-income birth ranges from $93 in 1970 to $286 in 1975.

A conservative estimate of the average government expenditure for maternity and first-year pediatric care associated with a birth to a low-income or marginal-income woman between 1970 and 1975 is provided by adding the two annual estimates from tables D.2 and D.3. These totals (shown in Table 7.2) are used in the computations of savings in chapter 7.

COSTS OF PUBLIC ASSISTANCE AND SELECTED SERVICES

Table D.4 assembles the information needed to estimate the annual costs to government of a birth to a public assistance recipient. These include the average annual cash payment and related administrative costs, and the average

TABLE D.1
Estimated Average Costs of Maternity and Pediatric Care During Infant's First Year for Low-Income and Marginal-Income Women: 1967–75

Year	Physicians' Fee Component of Consumer Price Index (1)	Cost of Physicians' Services ($)[a] (2)	Hospital Component of Consumer Price Index (3)	Cost of Hospital Services ($)[b] (4)	Total Cost ($) (2 + 4)
1967	100.0	247.64	100.0	454.02	701.66
1968	105.6	261.51	113.6	515.77	777.28
1969	112.9	279.59	128.8	584.78	864.37
1970	121.4	300.63	145.4	660.15	960.78
1971	129.8	321.44	163.1	740.51	1,061.95
1972	133.8	331.34	173.9	789.54	1,120.88
1973	138.2	342.24	182.1	826.77	1,169.01
1974	150.9	373.69	201.5	914.85	1,288.54
1975	169.4	419.50	236.1	1,071.94	1,490.94

[a] Based on 1970–71 cost of $311.04, at CPI value of 125.6 (average of 1970 and 1971 values).

[b] Based on 1970–71 cost of $700.56 at CPI value of 154.3 (average of 1970 and 1971 values).

Sources: Cols. 1 and 3 from *Statistical Abstract of the United States* (Washington, D.C.: U.S. Government Printing Office, 1975), Table 688, p.423; 1975 figures in cols. 1 and 3 from Bureau of Labor Statistics, February 1976.

TABLE D.2

Approximation of Government's Share of Hospital Maternity and Pediatric Costs for Low-Income and Marginal-Income Women: 1970-75

Category	1970	1971	1972	1973	1974	1975
1. Total government hospital costs ($ million)	14,018	16,465	18,019	20,061	23,483(e)	28,179 (e)
a. Less programs not applicable to maternity and pediatric care for low-income and marginal-income persons	8,049	9,316	10,386	11,510	13,386(e)	16,062 (e)
b. Programs applicable to maternity and pediatric care (public assistance vendor payments, general hospital and medical care, maternal and child health)	5,969	7,149	7,633	8,551	10,097(e)	12,117 (e)
2. Maternity admissions as percent of all hospital admissions	11.1	10.6	9.7	9.0	8.6	8.6(e)
3. Estimated cost to government of maternity admissions ($ million) (1b x 2)	662.6	757.8	740.4	769.6	868.3	1,042.1
4. a. Average hospital cost per low-income and marginal-income birth ($)	660	741	790	827	915	1,072
b. Estimated number of low-income and marginal-income births (1,000)	1,679	1,600	1,466	1,412	1,425	1,418
c. Total cost of hospital maternity and pediatric care for low-income and marginal-income births ($ million) (4a x 4b)	1,108.1	1,185.6	1,158.1	1,167.7	1,303.9	1,520.1
5. a. Governmental percent of total hospital cost (3÷4c)	59.8	63.9	63.9	65.9	66.6	68.6
b. Governmental share of total hospital cost per low-income and marginal-income birth ($) (4a x 5a)	395	473	505	545	609	735

(e) = estimated data.

Sources: Category 1 1970 from Social Security Administration, *Research and Statistics Note* no. 3, February 6, 1974, Table 3; 1971-73 from Social Security Administration, *Research and Statistics Note* no. 1, February 19, 1975, Table 3; 1974-75 are estimates based on aggregate governmental expenditures for hospital care reported for fiscal years 1974 and 1975 in Social Security Administration, *Research and Statistics Note* no. 20, November 21, 1975, Table 2, and 1971-73 trends in ratio of applicable programs to total expenditures. Category 2—derived from American Hospital Association, *Guide to the Health Care Field-1975 edition*, Table 1, p. 17; percent for 1975 is estimated. Category 4a—from Table D.1. Category 4b—based on estimate that women below 200 percent of poverty bear about 45 percent of all U.S. births, the proportion of all children under one year to women below 200 percent of poverty in the 1970 census. Births for 1970-74 from *Statistical Abstract of the United States* (Washington, D.C.: U.S. Government Printing Office, 1975), Table 67, p. 51; births for 1975 from *Monthly Vital Statistics Report*, 24 (12), March 4, 1976.

TABLE D.3

Approximation of Government's Share of Physicians' Costs for Maternity and Pediatric Care for Low-Income and Marginal-Income Women: 1970–75

Category	1970	1971	1972	1973	1974	1975
1. Total government expenditures for physicians' services ($ million)	3,238	3,463	3,813	4,209	5,296(e)	6,545(e)
a. Less programs not applicable to maternity and pediatric care for low-income and marginal-income persons	2,459	2,544	2,770	3,002	3,744(e)	4,516(e)
b. Programs applicable to maternity and pediatric care for low-income and marginal-income persons (public assistance medical care, general hospital and medical care, maternal and child health, Office of Economic Opportunity)	779	919	1,043	1,207	1,552	2,029(e)
2. Visits for maternity and pediatric care of low-income and marginal-income persons as percent of total physicians' visits (estimate)	20	20	20	20	20	20
3. Estimated cost to government of physicians' services for maternity and pediatric care of low-income and marginal-income persons ($ million) (1b x 2)	155.8	183.8	208.6	241.4	310.4	405.8
4. a. Average physician cost per low-income and marginal-income birth ($)	301	321	331	342	374	420
b. Estimated number of low-income and marginal-income births	1,679	1,600	1,466	1,412	1,425	1,418
c. Total cost of physicians' services for maternity and pediatric care of low-income and marginal-income births ($ million) (4a x 4b)	505.4	513.6	485.2	482.9	533.0	595.6
5. a. Government percent of total cost of physicians' services (3÷4c)	30.8	35.8	43.0	50.0	58.2	68.1
b. Government share of total cost of physicians' services per low-income and marginal-income birth ($) (4a x 5a)	93	115	142	171	218	286

(e) = estimated data.

Sources: Category 1 1970 from Social Security Administration, *Research and Statistics Note* no. 3, February 6, 1974, Table 3; 1971–73 from Social Security Administration, *Research and Statistics Note* no. 1, February 19, 1975, Table 3; 1974–75 are estimates based on aggregate governmental expenditures for physicians' services reported for fiscal years 1974 and 1975 in Social Security Administration, *Research and Statistics Note* no. 20, November 21, 1975, Table 2, and 1971–73 trends in ratio of applicable programs to total expenditures. Category 2—estimated from preliminary data from 1973 National Ambulatory Care Survey made available by the National Center for Health Statistics; the survey showed that 16.7 percent of all physician visits by blacks were to obstetrician-gynecologists and pediatricians. For low-income and marginal-income women, this proportion was increased to 20 percent on the assumption that a significant proportion of visits to general practitioners and family physicians are for maternity and pediatric care. Category 4a—from Table D.1. Category 4b—based on estimate that women below 200 percent of poverty bear about 45 percent of all U.S. births, the proportion of all children under one year to women below 200 percent of poverty in the 1970 census. Births for 1970–74 from *Statistical Abstract of the United States* (Washington, D.C.: U.S. Government Printing Office, 1975), Table 67, p. 51; births for 1975 estimated from *Monthly Vital Statistics Report*, 24 (12), March 4, 1976.

148

TABLE D.4
Estimated Annual Costs of Public Assistance and Selected Services per AFDC Recipient: 1970-75

Category	1970	1971	1972	1973	1974	1975
1. Number of AFDC recipients (1,000)	9,659	10,653	11,069	10,814	11,006	11,270
2. Average annual payment ($)	600	624	648	684	792	804
3. Estimated 10% administrative costs ($)	60.00	62.40	64.80	68.40	79.20	80.40
4. Expenditures for social services for AFDC recipients ($ million)	641.7	855.5	1,944.0	2,076.3	2,416.5	2,610.0
5. Average annual social service expenditure per AFDC recipient ($) (4÷1)	66.44	80.31	175.63	192.00	219.56	231.59
6. Expenditures for food stamps for AFDC recipients ($ million)*	346.1	937.1	1,190.0	1,347.8	1,663.1	2,247.4
7. Average annual food stamp expenditure per AFDC recipient ($) (6÷1)	35.83	87.97	107.51	124.63	151.11	199.41
8. Expenditures for federal food program for needy for AFDC recipients ($ million)	172.0	170.7	169.8	148.9	120.8	56.4
9. Average annual food program expenditure per AFDC recipient ($) (8÷1)	17.81	16.03	15.34	13.77	10.98	5.00
10. Public housing expenditures for AFDC recipients ($ million)	115.0	152.1	182.8	275.5	308.3	364.0
11. Average annual public housing expenditure per AFDC recipient ($) (11÷1)	11.91	14.28	16.51	25.48	28.01	32.30
12. Total average annual costs per AFDC recipient ($) (2+3+5+7+9+11)	791.99	884.99	1,027.79	1,108.28	1,280.86	1,352.70

(e) = estimated data.

*Federal administrative costs are included, but state and local government administrative costs are excluded. 1975 data are preliminary.

Sources: Category 1—1970–74, *Statistical Abstract of the United States* (Washington, D.C.: U.S. Government Printing Office, 1975), Table 486, p. 304; for 1975, DHEW, *Public Assistance Statistics*, July 1975, Tables 3 and 4. Category 2—based on average monthly payments reported in sources for Category 1. Category 4—figures are 90 percent of total expenditures for social services reported in *Statistical Abstract of the United States* (1975), Table 447, p. 281 (for 1970, 1972–74), and *Statistical Abstract of the United States* (1973), Table 461, p. 287 (for 1971); 1975 total is estimated (the 90 percent estimate was made by DHEW Social and Rehabilitation Service in 1974). Category 6—based on annual tables showing total participants, public assistance participants, and total federal costs prepared by Food and Nutrition Service, U.S. Department of Agriculture. Category 8—derived from data in *Statistical Abstract of the United States* (1975), Table 152, p. 93 (for 1970–74) and from preliminary data from Food and Nutrition Service, U.S. Department of Agriculture (for 1975). Category 10—figures are 25 percent of total expenditures for public housing reported in A.M. Skolnik and S.R. Dales, "Social Welfare Expenditures, Fiscal Year 1974," *Social Security Bulletin*, January 1976, Table 1; and their "Social Welfare Expenditures 1950–75" *Social Security Bulletin*, January 1976, Table 1. The 25 percent estimate is based on Joint Economic Committee, U.S. Congress, *Public Income Transfer Programs: The Incidence of Multiple Benefits and the Issues Raised by Their Receipt* (Washington, D.C.: U.S. Government Printing Office, 1972), Table 8, p. 26.

cost per Aid to Families with Dependent Children (AFDC) recipient of social services, food stamps and other food programs, and public housing. Omitted are several other large public programs that serve public assistance recipients as well as other low-income persons, such as child welfare, antipoverty programs, and institutional care. The resulting costs are thus understated; they range from $792 per AFDC birth in 1970 to $1,351 in 1975.

These costs, of course, can be applied only to those family planning patients who are public assistance recipients; between 1970 and 1975 they constituted 16 to 19 percent of the total family planning caseload. These costs per AFDC birth are translated into savings per birth averted among all family planning patients in Table 7.3.

NOTES

1. The previous studies are C. Muller and F. S. Jaffe, "Financing fertility related health services in the United States, 1972–1978: a preliminary projection," *Family Planning Perspectives,* 4:6, January 1972; and F. S. Jaffe, "Short-term costs and benefits of United States family planning programs," *Studies in Family Planning,* 5:98, March 1974. Data sources included the National Center for Health Statistics, the American College of Obstetricians and Gynecologists, the American Hospital Association, the American Medical Association, Blue Cross, and the Commission on Professional and Hospital Activities, complemented by local data obtained in an intensive study of Jacksonville, Florida.

PHILLIPS CUTRIGHT, Professor of Sociology at Indiana University, has specialized in studies of human fertility for the past decade. He has taught sociology at several universities and also conducted research at the U.S. Social Security Administration and the Joint Center for Urban Studies at MIT-Harvard Universities.

Professor Cutright received his Ph.D. from the University of Chicago and is the author of numerous articles on the family and fertility in such journals as *American Sociological Review, Demography, Population Studies, Family Planning Perspectives, Journal of Marriage and the Family, Social Biology,* and *Journal of Biosocial Science.*

FREDERICK S. JAFFE is President of The Alan Guttmacher Institute and Vice President of the Planned Parenthood Federation of America, with which he has been associated since 1954. During this period, he has been a close observer of, and participant in, the changes in public policy on family planning which permitted the current U.S. program to be developed during the 1960s. In 1967, he served as one of three consultants invited by the Department of Health, Education and Welfare to evaluate U.S. family planning efforts, and from 1970–72 he served as a special consultant to the Commission on Population Growth and the American Future.

He is a coauthor (with A. F. Guttmacher and W. Best) of *Birth Control and Love* (New York: Macmillan, 1969), and (with R. O. Greep and M. Koblinsky) *Reproduction and Human Welfare: A Challenge to Research* (Cambridge: MIT Press, 1976 forthcoming). He is also the author of more than two dozen articles dealing with family planning and population policy issues in such journals as *Science, Demography, Studies in Family Planning, Journal of Social Issues, Scientific American, Journal of the American Public Health Association,* and *Family Planning Perspectives.*

Mr. Jaffe was graduated from Queens College in 1947.

THE MICRO-ECONOMICS OF DEMOGRAPHIC CHANGE: Family
Planning and Economic Well-Being
Theodore K. Ruprecht and
Frank I. Jewett

POPULATION POLICIES FOR ECONOMIC DEVELOPMENT
edited by Michael C. Keeley